"The cavern of forgivenes:
Tracie's baby-step approac
The ease and simplicity o
room to respond to God's
Him."

~ Cassi Werner

"Tracie's 31 Days of Forgiveness had me at Bonus Chapter 1 –
'He Deserves What He Has Coming to Him.' Strong words
my entire family felt when the man who killed my 88 year old
uncle was sentenced to 23 years in prison. What a relief, we
can all breathe easier, right? I thought I had truly forgiven this
man, but after reading this chapter and book, I realized that was
NOT the case. I still wanted him to 'pay.' I realized God was
still working in my life when I sent Tracie a text telling her that
chapter really hit home for me. When Tracie shared she had
secretly written that chapter for me and my daughter, Marissa,
tears immediately started falling as I realized that I had not truly
forgiven this man, or other in my life for that matter, the way
God wanted me to. 1 John 3:15 – Anyone who hates another
brother or sister is really a murderer at heart. Thank you Tracie
for truly opening my eyes and my heart to Jesus' way!"

~ Lisa Mahnke

"The concept of forgiveness is so counter-culture. In a world
obsessed with scandal and how people hurt each other, this
book provides the escalator to lift you away from the pain, anger,
confusion and alienation."

~ Amy Schaefer

"I cannot think of anyone who would not benefit from reading
31 Days of Forgiveness by Tracie Stier-Johnson. If we are honest
with ourselves, brutally honest, we all deal with the subject of
forgiveness in some way, shape or form. We all have hurts and
we all have places in us that we need to dig deeper, as this study
does, to really seek out the peace that true forgiveness brings.
This 31 day series will give you the tools, Scriptures, prayers and

encouragement to dig in and search our hearts on the subject of forgiveness."

~ Candace Crabtree, MercyIsNew.com

"This is THE forgiveness manual. After reading 31 Days of Forgiveness I will never look at my relationships in the same way again. My eyes have been open to the beauty of forgiveness."

~ Angela Statzer, ButtonBirdDesigns.com

"Of all the subjects I was most afraid to explore, Forgiveness topped the list. Why should I learn how to forgive people who had legitimately wronged me? Imagine my surprise to learn that Forgiveness is a gift to myself first. Tracie does a thorough and compassionate job of helping you understand why we are compelled to forgive and what the true benefits are in doing so! I'm so grateful to have read this book!"

~ Su Rankin

"I didn't think I had any issues with forgiveness, but realized while reading 31 Days of Forgiveness I didn't really understand what forgiveness and grace really mean. The insight and wisdom you gave me is so helpful. I never understood the Prodigal Son. I never agreed with the father in the story and just chalked it up as something I would have to ask God about when I get to heaven...but you explained it in such a way that I get it now and really understand the depths of the parable!"

~ Marisa Ramsier, EnjoyingEachMoment.com

"I am amazed at how 31 Days of Forgiveness has affected my life and my relationship with God; it has already helped me save a friendship that I felt for sure had been destroyed. Thank you Tracie, for your insight, your wisdom, and your heart...you are a true gift."

~ Stephanie Morrell

"A book written truly from the heart and written to make you feel like Tracie is talking directly to you. During the 31 days of reading, if you open your heart, you will find such a peace when you reach the end. Your eyes will be opened to many hurts that you may not even be aware that you are holding on to and you will learn how to let them go and forgive. You will have a heart filled with God's love and a new way of dealing with new hurts that may come your way."

~ Martha Weber-Ross

"Not only is forgiveness God's commandment to us, it frees us from the unhealthy by-products of unforgiveness such as anger, grudge holding, and stress. Tracie teaches us the tools to forgive."

~ Lori Bartynski

"I don't now about anyone else but the stronger my faith, the harder I find it to forgive myself for mistakes I have made. Tracie's book, 31 days of forgiveness is a great tool to help through the process of forgiveness of others as well as yourself. I found the study guide a great way for me to reflect and really work through my feelings to open myself to a greater relationship with God. Thank you Tracie!"

~ MKS

"Forgiveness. A lack of it can wreck your life. Embracing it will set you free to live radically transformed. In 31 Days of Forgiveness, Tracie Stier-Johnson, tackles the subject with the voice of a warm-hearted friend and the passion of a woman who knows this journey personally. Her 31 day format invites you into experience lessons steeped in relevant, biblical truth and her simple words open the door for a personal response. Tracie's book will be one I'll add to my resource library and recommend to those desiring to life a life of impact."

~ Elisa Pulliam, Life Coach, Mentor
& Author – ElisaPulliam.com, MoreToBe.com

"I didn't realize I was holding on to 'unforgiveness', but as I worked my way through this book, one day at a time, it became clear that I needed to let go of those grudges I wasn't even aware I was holding. I now view my relationships with others in a new light, and I pray that they too will come to find the comfort I have discovered through truly forgiving."

~ Misty Thieman, EncouragingSweetness.blogspot.com

"The truths of what forgiveness is and is not. As I read about these, I felt God open a window and let in fresh air. I breathed in the grace of His truths and exhaled all my preconceptions. I'm so thankful to Tracie for sharing these life words and setting me on my amazing journey of freedom with God."

~ Jeri Taira

31 days
of forgiveness
{through the eyes of grace}

Tracie Stier-Johnson

Copyright Information

Cover design: Design by Insight {www.designbyinsight.net}

Editor: Sandra Peoples, Next Step Editing {www.nextstepediting.com}

ISBN-10: 1482091615

ISBN-13: 978-1482091618

All proceeds of 31 Days of Forgiveness will go to

The Seed Company (theseedcompany.com)

Today, nearly one-third

of the world's language groups,

representing 350 million people,

are still waiting for God's Word

in a language they can understand clearly.

The Seed Company enables you

to support local Bible translators

as they make God's message available

in the language of their people.

Taylor Rio

You have taught me much
about forgiveness and grace.
My prayer is for you to continue
to shine Jesus all the days of your life.

Table of Contents

Bonus Chapters

Introduction

You know how God prepares us for something? We may not know it at the time, but as the days, weeks, months, and years pass we can look back and say, "Ahhhh, so that's what God had up His sleeve!"

Over the last few years, I've walked many of the afore mentioned situations. And they were painful. And I hated every minute. Until I began to realize they were all for a purpose.

As I grew in my faith and my belief that God was refining me, I was able to face my trials head on and with joy. My e-book, 31 Days of Faith {finding joy in your anguish},[1] came out of that journey. I was able to use my pain to eventually encourage others.

And so it is with 31 Days of Forgiveness {through the eyes of grace}. God has put me in many situations requiring more forgiveness and grace than I'm humanly able to give.

Looking back, I can say I'm thankful—not of the situation, but of the lessons learned—for what I've walked through. I've become passionate about radical forgiveness and grace. And I believe the Lord has called me to walk the path I have so I could turn back and encourage others.

Then the Lord said, "Simon, Simon, listen! Satan has demanded to have you apostles for himself.

He wants to separate you from me as a farmer

separates wheat from husks. But I have prayed for
you,

Simon, that your faith will not fail. So when you
recover,

strengthen the other disciples."

Luke 22:31-32 {GOD'S WORD}

Friends, we are called to use our God-given stories for His glory.

We are called to live lives pleasing to our Creator. We are called to imitate Christ. We are called to be salt and light {Matthew 5:13-16}.

We're not called to do just the things we want to do. Or just the things that come easy to us.

Dying on a cross did not come easy to Jesus, and as we'll explore in upcoming chapters, He didn't want to do it either.

Forgiveness is one of the hardest things we're called to do. And dying on a cross for our sins was one of the hardest things Jesus had to do.

But He did it anyway. For us. So we could live redeemed, forgiven, and free.

If we accept this gift from Him on a daily basis, who are we to keep it? Why are we not extending this same gift to others?

The very message of the cross is forgiveness, flowing from God's grace. When we keep what we've been given, we are no longer sharing the message of the cross.

Are you harboring unforgiveness, bitterness, resentment, or anger? It hurts doesn't it? But do you know we don't have to live that way?

As much as I believe I'm living out a life of forgiveness, writing this series has rocked my world. Rocked. Upside-down rocked. In a totally good way, I promise! As I was researching, and reading, and digging, and diving deeply into the Word of God . . . He changed me in a way I didn't see coming.

And I know He'll do the same for you.

Do you know "unforgiveness" isn't even in the dictionary? Let's not hold on to something that isn't even a word!

As we take this journey of forgiveness, my prayer and belief is that you'll come around to a new way of thinking. You'll begin to see your situation and circumstances through the eyes of Christ . . . through the eyes of grace.

Stay the course friends . . . keep your hearts and minds open to this journey. If you do, I promise you, your life will never be the same.

In Him,

Tracie

A Prayer for Forgiveness
{day one}

*Then make me truly happy by agreeing
wholeheartedly with each other,*

*loving one another, and working together with
one mind and purpose.*

Philippians 2:2 {NLT}

Friends, I'm thrilled you're joining me for this series! My very first thoughts in this journey have me thinking of the 1965 song, "What the World Needs Now" {is love, sweet love}.

What the world needs right now is a whole lotta forgiveness. Honest-to-goodness, godly forgiveness.

Not the fluffy stuff.

But the hard stuff.

The stuff with seeds of anger and bitter roots.

Over the next 31 days we're going to dig into the hard stuff until we've unearthed and bared the deepest part of our souls.

But before we can go any further . . . let's start this journey with prayer to soften our hearts and minds, asking God to work mightily in our lives. You can use the following prayer, or use your own.

Father,

I open my heart to You. I'm fully committing to emptying my heart of any anger, bitterness, or unforgiveness residing there. Lord, soften and purify my heart through this journey and show me where I'm holding on to any resentments. Help me to surrender and give it all to you. I admit I can no longer hold on to the pain, help me release it to You.

Lord, as I read through this study over the next month, I ask for a heart of grace. Help me to see my situation and circumstances through the eyes of grace.

Lord, help me to walk in love and in peace. Help me to love others as You love them. Help me to forgive as You forgave.

Thank you Father for hearing my prayer and knowing my heart.

In Your loving name I pray,

Amen

Friends, if you find at any point in this forgiveness journey you're struggling or questioning, could you keep this prayer in mind? If you've got some hard things going on, might I even suggest you start each day of this series by coming back to this prayer and praying it again and again.

I promise . . . if you let God work in your heart over the next month . . . your life will never be the same.

What Is Forgiveness?
{day two}

God's forgiveness is not just a casual statement;

it is the complete blotting out of all dirt and

degradation of our past, present, and future.

~ Billy Graham

Before we dive in deep, let's spend the next few days exploring the definition of forgiveness, why we should forgive, what forgiveness looks like, and then we'll talk about how we can forgive.

The word forgive is defined as a verb. *The New Oxford American Dictionary* defines the word forgive this way, "stop feeling angry or resentful toward (someone) for an offense, flaw, or mistake." It is also defined as, "cancel (a debt)."

The word "cancel" is also a verb. So in order for us to forgive and cancel, it requires an action from us. Not from the other person, but from us. These words are also used to describe cancel: decide; annul or revoke; abolish or make void.

Those definitions tell me when we decide to forgive it requires action on our part. And in my dictionary, I'd also list the caveat of "requires a lot of prayer!"

What kind of action does forgiveness require? The action of prayer, the action of ceasing our angry, bitter, or resentful feelings, and the action of canceling.

- Forgiveness is a hard thing to offer. We need to be prayerful in each situation, asking God to open and soften our hearts, seeking His heart and asking for His help. In our human power, forgiveness is often times impossible.

- Forgiveness requires we stop feeling angry, bitter, or resentful. Through prayer and a deep belief or conviction, it truly is possible to stop these venomous feelings.

- Lastly, forgiveness requires us to cancel the debt. We need to prayerfully choose to annul, revoke, abolish, and make void whatever act requires forgiveness from us. If we cancel a debt {forgive}, we keep no record of the wrongdoing and rid ourselves of any feelings of vengeance.

Ultimately, forgiveness is grace . . . a free and unmerited {not deserved} favor. Often times, in our minds, forgiveness isn't deserved. But true forgiveness, a heart forgiveness, forgives anyway.

The bottom line, and the heart behind this series, as Christians—Christ followers—we've been commanded to forgive others as we've been forgiven. More on that in the coming days, but for now let's reflect on this question:

How can we take what's been given to us on the cross and keep it? Forgiveness was given to us that we might give it away.

As hard as it might be, I've learned I can only give what's been given to me on the cross.

What Forgiveness Is Not
{day three}

Once a woman has forgiven her man,

she must not reheat his sins for breakfast.

~ Marlene Dietrich

In order to truly forgive, in the way God intends us to forgive, and with a pure heart, we need to understand and check our motives. Raise your hand if you've ever read or heard a message and thought, "Oh how I wish so-and-so were here for this message, she SO needs it!" I admit my hand is {humbly} raised.

Many times we do things with the wrong motives and heart. Sometimes intentionally, but most times we're not even aware. We truly desire to make a situation better and innocently think the situation would get better if the other person could "get" the message too!

Feel me?

So before we move any further, and in an attempt to purify our own hearts, let's explore what forgiveness is not.

- *Forgiveness is not expecting someone to acknowledge her wrongdoing*
  The fact is, someone may not know she's hurt us, she may not care she's hurt us, and we may never see or speak to her again. But we're required to forgive regardless. True story.

- *Forgiveness is not enabling, excusing, condoning, or justifying sin*
  God forgives us without approving of our sin. We're required to do the same. Forgiveness loves despite sin. We'll discuss this further in the upcoming days.

- *Forgiveness is not reconciliation*
  As mentioned above, you may have to forgive someone who you'll never see again. Or after forgiving him, you might not want a close relationship with him . . . or he may have walked away from you. Reconciliation is restoration of a relationship and takes both parties to want a restored relationship. Quite honestly, reconciliation might not be possible.

- *Forgiveness is not forgetting*
  Although we may not be able to forget, we can choose to keep no record of the wrongdoing. We'll go into this in greater detail over the next few weeks.

- *Forgiveness is not a one-time event*
  If we've been deeply hurt, even if we've chosen to forgive, the offense will most likely surface from time-to-time. And just because we've forgiven doesn't mean we're covered for life. We may have to make a conscious effort again and again to forgive.

Father, help us to look at our own hearts and not point our fingers toward our neighbors. Help us to understand the true meaning of forgiveness and enter in with pure hearts.

Why Do We Need to Forgive?
{day four}

*If you forgive those who sin against you, your
heavenly Father will forgive you.*

*But if you refuse to forgive others, your Father
will not forgive your sins.*

Matthew 6:14-15 {NLT}

That Scripture right there is pretty black and white in my book. Forgive, or you won't be forgiven. That's the bottom line. We've been commanded to forgive.

And if we don't? Every.single.sin. we commit won't be forgiven either. Woah!

That doesn't mean only the big sins—remember, a sin is a sin— God doesn't hold one more accountable than another.

Murder? In our book, big sin.

Gossip? In our book, small sin.

In God's book? Equal.

I saw a great quote on Pinterest that reads, "Don't judge someone just because they sin differently than you."

It's important to note, not only are there biblical reasons why we should forgive, there are significant health benefits as well. An online article from Mayo Clinic[2] had this to say:

Forgiveness brings a kind of peace that helps us go on with life. Letting go of grudges and bitterness can make way for compassion, kindness, and peace. Forgiveness can lead to:

- Healthier relationships
- Greater spiritual and psychological well-being
- Less anxiety, stress, and hostility
- Lower blood pressure
- Fewer symptoms of depression
- Lower risk of alcohol and substance abuse

Looks to me like we have two very important reasons to forgive ... because God has commanded us to, and because we can lead healthier—physically and spiritually—lives if we do.

Lastly, unforgiveness is like having shackles and chains around our emotions and lives. Unforgiveness controls us, while forgiveness enables us to create our own life paths.

Forgiveness brings freedom. Freedom from what binds us. Freedom to let go. Freedom to move on. And freedom to live fully and abundantly, the way God intended.

> *The thief comes only to steal and kill and destroy.*
>
> *I came that they may have life and have it abundantly.*
>
> *John 10:10 {ESV}*

Ultimately, forgiveness is a choice. A choice to live bound. Or a choice to live free.

The question remains, which do we want and which will we choose?

How Do We Forgive?
{day five}

To be a Christian means to forgive the inexcusable
because
God has forgiven the inexcusable in you.
~ C.S. Lewis

We left off yesterday asking which we'd choose . . . unforgiveness and living bound, or forgiveness and living free? Since you're back here with me today, I'm guessing you've chosen to live free. I know I have!

So now to answer the biggie . . . how in the world do we forgive!? We've been betrayed, lied to, stolen from, wronged, talked about, abused, abandoned, and the list {sadly} goes on.

Extending true forgiveness is probably one of the hardest things we're called to do in this life. And there certainly isn't a magic formula to get there. But what I intend to do over the next month is share many different perspectives, references, Scriptures, thoughts, and my own experiences to help you begin the admittedly difficult process of forgiveness.

As I mentioned, forgiveness is an act of grace. The very definition of grace is giving to someone what isn't deserved. That's an incredibly hard concept to wrap our heads around, especially when we're victims of the afore mentioned "crimes."

Do I have your heart on the "why" we need to forgive? And what forgiveness is not? Before we proceed with this, let's take a little check of our spirits to be sure our hearts are wide open to receiving this message {and the messages in the days that follow}.

As Gandhi so wisely said, "We need to be the change we want to see." How many of us want the other person to apologize first? Hand raised! But we need to understand forgiveness needs to start with us.

We also need to understand forgiveness doesn't just start with us . . . it's possible it may end with us too. We may never see change on the other side of forgiveness {from the other person}. But remember the key truth—forgiveness is for us, not the other person.

That said, let's take a look at Jesus in the garden of Gethsemane. The story is found in all the Gospels, but unless noted, I'm using text from Matthew 26:36-46.

Knowing what the next day would hold for Him, Jesus said to His disciples, "My soul is overwhelmed with sorrow to the point of death." Verse 39 says, "Going a little further, he fell with his face to the ground and prayed, 'My Father, if it is possible may this cup be taken from me. Yet not as I will, but as you will.'"

Let me put this bluntly. The very next day, Jesus would die a horrific and painful death. Why? For our sins. So we could be forgiven.

And guess what friends? He didn't wanna do it! Simply put, He didn't feel like it. Never before had He asked His Father to take something from Him, but this time . . . He didn't wanna do it.

I'm humbled when I think of the sacrifice. Luke 22:44 tells us, "And being in anguish, he prayed more earnestly, and his sweat was like drops of blood falling to the ground."

Oh how I urge you to take a few minutes to reflect on what He did for us! Starting that night in the garden, the betrayals, the mocking, the beatings—hanging broken on a cross.

All for our forgiveness.

Sure we might say, "But you don't know what was done to me." And I get that. I've been there. There've been countless times I just don't wanna forgive.

But I'd argue this, any "crime" committed against me is nothing compared to an innocent man taking on my sins, for my freedom and my forgiveness on a cross. Nothing.

Can I pose a challenge? What if, the next time we're struggling to forgive, we visualize Jesus, broken, bloody, and beaten, hanging on the cross so that our sins {however big, or however little in our minds} might be forgiven?

I wonder, knowing what's been done for us, how can we not extend forgiveness to others?

> *". . . be kind to each other, tenderhearted,*
> *forgiving one another,*
> *just as God through Christ has forgiven you."*
> *Ephesians 4:32 {NLT}*

Be Quick to Forgive
{day six}

Forgiveness must be immediate, whether or not a person asks for it.

~ Rick Warren

The easiest way to forgive? Make it a way of life. Let forgiveness be part of our makeup, part of our DNA, and our character {who we are when no one's looking}.

Let us fully commit to understanding why we need to forgive. When we can approach forgiveness with pure hearts and no "yeah buts" . . . forgiveness *will* start to become a part of our DNA. I'm living proof of that.

Truth is, it isn't always easy and sometimes I really don't want to forgive. But the more I understand I'm required to forgive the easier it becomes.

And the easier it becomes, the easier it is to forgive immediately. Because friends, if we don't learn to forgive immediately, a bitter seed is planted and roots of bitterness start to grow.

Do not be bitter or angry or mad. Never shout angrily or

say things to hurt others. Never do anything evil.

Ephesians 4:31 {NCV}

I pray we use this study to prepare our hearts that we might live tenderheartedly toward others. Let's think of our hearts in the way a garden is prepared . . . please let it be said I'm the last person considered a garden authority . . . but what little I ~~Googled~~ do know, just might serve us well here.

As one would prepare a garden or flowerbed, the first step is to prepare the ground for planting by turning the soil, pulling weeds, and making sure there's proper drainage. When proper preparation is done, the garden has a greater chance to produce a bountiful crop. The opposite holds true, if the right preparation isn't done, the garden is likely to die.

How does this apply to us?

- *Prepare the ground {our hearts}* – through this study, through prayer, through understanding

- *Turn the soil* – spend some time in prayer discovering what's hiding in our hearts

- *Pull out any weeds* – unresolved bitterness and unforgiveness

- *Proper drainage* – to drain is to empty out. Let us commit to hearts that empty out any ugly things that could take root, and replace them with things that are holy, pure, and righteous.

Nothing good will come of holding onto unforgiveness and bitterness. It's a poison that will eat us alive if we let it.

Here's a scenario to ponder:

There are two siblings of the same sex. As very young children, their mother up and leaves them. No word, no warning, just leaves. The children are left with their dad, who remarries a woman who isn't too fond of her new stepchildren and treats them poorly into their teen years. Sadly, their father never stepped in to help his children.

32

As we follow one sibling, we notice anger, rebellion, bitterness, pessimism, and the-world-owes-me mentality. Bottom line is, this child is harboring unforgiveness and is seemingly living bound and shackled.

As we watch the other sibling, we see a loving, kind, tenderhearted, obedient, and strive-to-make-a-better-life-for-herself child. It seems this child hasn't let unforgiveness and bitterness rule her life. This child lives in freedom.

It's important to note in this story, the birth mother, father, and stepmother never asked for forgiveness. They never admitted to doing anything wrong. In fact, they were, most likely, oblivious to how deeply these children were being hurt.

We need to take note that even though forgiveness wasn't asked for, or a wrongdoing admitted to, the child who lives a life of forgiveness, lives a life of freedom.

As I write, I can literally feel these two children and their attitudes in my soul. When I think of the first, I feel heavy and sad. But when I think of the second, I feel weightless and free!

Shouldn't we always live weightless and free? It's our choice you know. God gave us free will to choose how we'd react to our life circumstances. Thankfully, He also gave us an instruction guide.

Get rid of all bitterness, rage, anger, harsh words,
and slander,

as well as all types of evil behavior. Instead, be
kind to

each other, tenderhearted, forgiving one another,

just as God through Christ has forgiven you.

Ephesians 4:31-32 {NLT}

Forgiveness Comes From Love
{day seven}

He who is devoid of the power to forgive, is devoid of the power to love.

~ Martin Luther King Jr.

There is Scripture after Scripture commanding us to love one another and the importance behind it. In my own personal life, I can attest to the power of love in forgiveness and how they are so intertwined.

I was faced with a seemingly hopeless situation requiring more forgiveness than a human is capable of. Instead of going down the path of bitterness, anger, and ugly . . . I prayed.

I prayed for, and was given to the point of overflowing, God's all-consuming love. When my prayer was literally, immediately answered and I was filled with His great love, I was able to offer it to a person, who in my own human eyes, was completely undeserving of it. Not only was he undeserving of my love, he was equally, if not more so, undeserving of my forgiveness.

But as God's love flowed through me, I was able to extend His love and ultimately, forgiveness to someone else. And because of this radical love, grace, and forgiveness, I was able to watch a hurting and broken person come to Christ.

Most important of all, continue to show deep love
for each other,
for love covers a multitude of sins.
1 Peter 4:8 {NLT}

You see friends, love and forgiveness aren't ours to hold on to. They're meant to share and give away. Redemption, freedom, and joy come when we live how we've been commanded to live.

In the gospel of Mark, we read an account where the teachers of the law ask Jesus, "Of all the commandments, which is the most important?"

"The most important one," answered Jesus, "is this . . . 'Love the Lord your God with all your heart and with all your soul and with all your mind and with all your strength.' The second is this: 'Love your neighbor as yourself.' There is no commandment greater than these."

Two gospels over, in John chapter 13, we read of the Last Supper. During that meal Jesus spoke to the disciples, explaining what would come, and leaving them with His last thoughts and commands. In verses 34 and 35, Jesus says, "A new command I give you: Love one another. As I have loved you, so you must love one another. By this all men will know that you are my disciples, if you love one another."

Watch what God does, and then you do it, like
children who
learn proper behavior from their parents.
Mostly what God does is love you. Keep company
with
him and learn a life of love. Observe how Christ
loved us.
His love was not cautious but extravagant.
He didn't love in order to get something from us

but to give everything of himself to us. Love like
that.

Ephesians 5:1-2 {MSG, emphasis mine}

Oh to love like that! Here's the thing . . . if we're walking and living life everyday with Christ, as the Scripture above tells us we should be doing, a love like that is not only possible, but also a way of life. It's something flowing through us that we're not even aware of. I'm the first to admit, loving and forgiving are not always easy, but I'm proof it's possible.

Matthew Henry says, "God is love; and those that dwell in love dwell in God and God in them."

The above Scripture says God's "love was not cautious, but extravagant." *The New Oxford American Dictionary* defines extravagant as "exceeding what is reasonable or appropriate; absurd."

God love has no "ifs." I'll love you *if* you promise to never-ever-never ever hurt me. I'll love you *if* I feel like it. I'll love you *if* you're loveable. I'll forgive *if* you ask for forgiveness. I'll forgive *if* you're really sorry and spend the rest of your life proving it to me.

God's love isn't cautious and has no restrictions. He doesn't love us to get something from us. God has loved us before we were ever born . . . extravagantly.

Can we love like that?

Love Comes from God
{day eight}

Dear friends, let us continue to love one another,

*for **love comes from God**. Anyone who loves is a*

child of God and knows God. But anyone who

does not love does not know God, for God is love.

1 John 4:7-8 {NLT, emphasis mine}

If we understand that forgiveness comes from a place of love and we've been commanded to love each other, let's go a layer deeper to understand that love comes from God.

It isn't humanly possible to know how much God loves us. How wide, long, high, and deep . . .

And may you have the power to understand, as all
God's people should,
how wide, how long, how high, and how deep his
love is.

May you experience the love of Christ,
though it is too great to understand fully.
Ephesians 3:18 {NLT, emphasis mine}

Paul, the author of Ephesians, goes on to say in verse 19, "Then you will be made complete with all the fullness of life and power that comes from God."

When we experience and try to understand the depths of His love for us, we'll be made complete with *all* the fullness of life and *power* that comes from God.

Forgiveness and love don't come from our strength. Maybe they do sometimes . . . "Mom, I'm sorry for that speeding ticket." "It's okay, I forgive you." And a lecture ensues.

But the hard stuff, the deep stuff, the painful stuff—power to forgive those things comes from God and God alone.

I love how Paul finishes his prayer for the Ephesians in verse 20, "Now all glory to God, who is able, through his mighty power at work within us, to accomplish infinitely more than we might ask or think."

There's a quote I've heard, "Have you prayed about it as much as you talk about it?" Ouch! Right? So let's ask ourselves if we're struggling with forgiveness, have we thought to pray about it? Asking God to work His mighty power within us and our situations?

His Word promises He'll accomplish *infinitely more* than what we might ask or think. When we ask for His help in forgiving or loving someone, He's able to give us *infinitely* more. Can you imagine the limitless power we have to forgive and love others?

I'm living proof to that testimony. It's not by my own strength, but by His . . . His wonderful, beautiful, limitless power flowing through me.

Give thanks to the God of heaven.
His faithful love endures forever.

Psalm 136:26 {NLT}

Radical Love, Radical Forgiveness, and Judgment
:: Part 1 ::
{day nine}

Unforgiveness denies the victim the possibility of parole and

leaves them stuck in the prison of what was, incarcerating

them in their trauma and relinquishing the chance

to escape beyond the pain.

~ Bishop T.D. Jakes

Jesus loves radically. Jesus forgives radically.

Radical is defined as thorough or complete. Let's continue reading today with the understanding we're talking about *thoroughly and completely* loving and forgiving.

There's a story in the Bible that moves me in a profound way each time I read it. The story can be found in John 8:3-11. It tells of a woman caught in the act of adultery and brought before Jesus for judgment.

It was dawn when Jesus appeared in the temple courts at the Mount of Olives. A crowd was gathered and Jesus sat before them to teach them. As Jesus began teaching, the teachers of the law brought the adulterous woman before Him, "Teacher," they said to Jesus, "this woman was caught in the act of adultery. The law of Moses says to stone her. What do you say?"

It's important to note it was dawn, she was caught in the act, and taken to Jesus while He was speaking in a public forum. Translation, she was most likely naked or wearing very little and standing before a large crowd, afraid and humiliated and *naked*.

The Bible says Jesus stooped to the ground to write something in the dust. There's no actual account of what He wrote. People, scholars, have taken guesses . . . my thought is He might've been buying some time before answering. Finally Jesus stood and said to them, "Anyone here who has never sinned can throw the first stone at her." And he bent to the ground again, writing in the dust.

The Bible goes on to say, "Those who heard Jesus began to leave one by one, first the older men and then the others. Jesus was left there alone with the woman standing before him. Jesus raised up again and asked her, 'Woman, where are they? Has no one judged you guilty?'

She answered, 'No one, sir.'

Then Jesus said, 'I also don't judge you guilty. You may go now, but don't sin anymore.'"

Come on . . . the woman was *clearly* guilty. She was caught in the act and was wearing the *naked* truth!

But Jesus . . . filled with love and forgiveness, didn't judge her guilty. His only request was that she didn't commit the sin again.

Let's take a minute to ask ourselves . . . if we were in the crowd that day and witnessed the events that took place, how would Jesus' decision affect us?

Before we answer these questions, think of a crime so huge the transgressor would deserve death. Realize, adultery in that day was a huge crime. A crime so big it deserved an immediate and painful death.

Would we agree, honor, and encourage others with His decision? Or would we be outraged and turn on Him {and the adulterer} with our own judgments?

Radical Love,
Radical Forgiveness,
and Judgment
:: Part 2 ::
{day ten}

Forgiveness does not exonerate the perpetrator.
Forgiveness liberates the victim. It's a gift you
give yourself. It has less to do with what somebody
else did as much as it does with your decision to
move on with your life and not be continually
victimized by rehearsing that issue or incident
over and over again.

~ Bishop T.D. Jakes

I read a People magazine online article[3] about a falsely accused former California high school football star. Brian Banks had hopes of an NFL career. Instead, the accusations of kidnap and rape when he was just sixteen years old, put him in jail for five years and labeled him a sex offender.

When the girl who falsely accused him reached out to admit she had lied ten years earlier, he gained his freedom and his name was cleared.

When Matt Lauer interviewed him on the Today show and asked if there were any consequences given to the accuser, Brian replied, "I haven't given it much thought."

When asked if he had any thoughts of revenge, "No," said Banks. "It's easy to have those feelings initially when you first hear the story. I've been dealing with this now for ten years, and I've had my moments where I was very angry, and very vengeful. But I know it was *best for me* to try and move forward in a positive manner, and for the *betterment of me. It hurts no one but myself* to hang onto that type of negative energy, and it will only *keep me in a stagnant position"* {emphasis mine}.

Amen Brian, Amen!

If faced with the same situation, I wonder how we'd react?

Based on the comments left on the article, it seems Brian's thoughts on forgiveness are in the minority. At the time of this writing, there are 216 comments and as I scrolled through just the first few pages of them, most all are full of judgment and hate to the woman who falsely accused Brian.

Here's a piece of one comment, "He's the better man for forgiving her though . . . I would slap her then sue her, and shame her into hiding. That's just me though. I think it's ridiculous how someone can accuse you of something you DID NOT DO, and get paid for it."

Most of them are very similar.

I was shocked. And angered. How can these people spew such hate and feel it's their right to judge? Sometimes the judgment of others hurts worse than the crime. I know this from personal experience.

The Bible tells us it's not our place to judge.

> *Don't pick on people, jump on their failures,*
> *criticize their faults—unless, of course, you want*
> *the same treatment. That critical spirit has a way*
> *of boomeranging. It's easy to see a smudge on your*

46

neighbor's face and be oblivious to the ugly sneer
on your own. Do you have the nerve to say, "Let
me wash your face for you," when your own face
is distorted by contempt? It's this whole traveling
road-show mentality all over again, playing a
holier-than-thou part instead of just living your
part. Wipe that ugly sneer off your own face,
and you might be fit to offer a washcloth to your
neighbor.

Matthew 7:1-5 {MSG}

Think about the passage we read yesterday about the adulterous woman whose crime deserved death by stoning as punishment. Instead Jesus said, "Anyone here who has never sinned can throw the first stone at her."

When everyone took a quick reflection of their own sins, they dropped their stones and walked away.

Friends, we are all sinners. Can't we too, drop our stones and leave judgment alone?

What Brian offered to his accuser is radical forgiveness. Could we offer the same?

Radical Love,
Radical Forgiveness,
and Judgment
:: Part 3 ::
{day eleven}

Justice and forgiveness can cohabitate.

Forgiveness does not have to compromise justice.

~ Bishop T.D. Jakes

Similar to yesterday's story, today I'd like to share three others.

The first is from a non-fiction book called, *Picking Cotton*, from author's Jennifer Thompson-Cannino and Ronald Cotton.

Following is a description from the back of the book:

> *Jennifer Thompson was raped at knifepoint by a man who broke into her apartment while she slept. She was able to escape, and eventually positively identified Ronald Cotton as her attacker. Ronald insisted that she was mistaken—but Jennifer's positive identification was the compelling evidence that put him behind bars. After eleven years, Ronald was allowed to take a DNA test that proved his innocence. He was*

released after serving more than a decade in
prison for a crime he never committed. Two years
later, Jennifer and Ronald met face-to-face—and
forged an unlikely friendship that changed both of
their lives.

In their own words, Jennifer and Ronald unfold
the harrowing details of their tragedy, and
challenge our ideas of memory and judgment
while demonstrating the profound nature
*of human grace and the **healing power of***
forgiveness.

In his review of the book John Grisham says, ". . . It is the powerful account of violence, rage, redemption, and ultimately, forgiveness."

Another powerful story of forgiveness . . . of forgiving the unforgiveable . . . comes to us in the non-fiction book, *The Devil in Pew Number Seven*, from author Rebecca Nichols Alonzo.

Following are excerpts from the back of the book:

Rebecca never felt safe as a child.

The first time the Nichols family received a
harassing phone call, they dismissed it. The same
went for the anonymous letter that threatened
they'd leave "crawling or walking . . . dead or
alive." But what they couldn't ignore was the
strategy of terror their tormentor unleashed, more
devastating and violent than they could have ever
imagined. Refusing to be driven away, Rebecca's
father stood his ground until one night when an
armed man walked into the family's kitchen . . .
and Rebecca's life was shattered.

If anyone had reason to harbor hatred and seek
personal revenge, it would be Rebecca. Yet The

50

Devil in Pew Number Seven tells a different
story. It is the amazing, true saga of relentless
persecution, one family's faith and courage in the
face of it, and a daughter whose parents taught her
the **power of forgiveness.**

There are numerous, inspiring quotes I could share from the
book, but here are just two passages that touched me the deepest:

". . . forgiveness is close to the heart of God.

. . . forgiveness is the language of heaven.

. . . forgiveness should be a way of life.

Even when it was humanly inconceivable to do so."

*"I think Momma would agree that I'm the keeper of the door to my
heart. To love and forgive others as I've been loved and forgiven by
Jesus, I have to guard what I allow to take root in my heart. If I open
my heart to self-pity, anger, grudges, and unforgiveness, I give the
enemy of my soul an invitation into a very expensive home—a home
purchased by the blood of Jesus. But as I become fluent in the language
of heaven, as I open the door of my heart to Jesus and in His strength
forgive others, that's when I'm set free."*

Just one more story I'd like to share is that of the infamous
Casey Anthony. The mother who was tried for the first degree
murder of her two-year old daughter, Caylee, but acquitted. I'm
assuming you know the story, as it made headlines around the
world.

What I remember most were all the Facebook and Twitter posts
spewing outrage, hate, and judgment at the verdict.

Honestly, I never followed the story. In full disclosure, I don't
read the paper or watch the news. Sure, I'd heard of the story, but
I never got emotionally involved, until I saw an episode of True

Hollywood Story airing the story. I'll admit, after watching the episode, one could definitely see how she might be guilty.

The part where I got emotionally involved? When they showed the hundreds and thousands of people who were outraged, full of judgment and hate outside the trial. Signs with hateful messages and chanting filled with judgment. Thinking about it bothers me all over again!

Friends, who are we to judge? We haven't walked Casey's path. *If* she truly is guilty—think about what she has to live with everyday. *If* she truly is guilty—we have no idea what could've happened in her life to cause her to commit such a crime.

What I know for sure is that people don't do unthinkable things just for the fun of it. People who commit heinous crimes are broken, hurting people who need to be loved. Who need a Savior. People who have God-shaped holes in their hearts.

Friends, the bottom line is, we didn't walk every day with Casey. We don't know if she's really guilty or not. The jury found her not guilty. Who are we to spew anything but understanding and grace. Truly.

God is the final judge. *If* she got away with something, it's her cross to bear and she'll have to answer to God one day.

And guess what? *We* also have to answer to God one day and the Bible tells us not to judge.

> *Do not judge others, and you will not be judged.*
> *For you will be treated as you treat others. The*
> *standard you use in judging is the standard by*
> *which you will be judged.*
>
> *Matthew 7:1-2 {NLT}*

*I saw the dead, both great and small, standing
before God's throne. And the books were opened,
including the Book of Life. And the dead were
judged according to what they had done, as
recorded in the books.*

Revelation 20:12 {NLT}

*Don't speak evil against each other, dear brothers
and sisters. If you criticize and judge each other,
then you are criticizing and judging God's law.
But your job is to obey the law, not to judge
whether it applies to you. God alone, who gave the
law, is the Judge. He alone has the power to save
or to destroy. So what right do you have to judge
your neighbor?*

James 4:11-12 {NLT}

Indeed. What right do we have to judge our neighbors?

Have you heard the Casting Crowns song, *"Jesus, Friend of
Sinners"*? I love it. Love every word of it. I'll share more thoughts
in a few days, but today would like to leave you with this verse
from the song:

*Nobody knows what we're for only against when
we judge the wounded*

*What if we put down our signs crossed over the
lines and loved like You did?*

Forgiving the Unforgivable
{day twelve}

Our Savior kneels down and gazes upon the
darkest acts of our lives. But rather than recoil in
horror, he reaches out in kindness and says, "I can
clean that if you want." And from the basin of his
grace, he scoops a palm full of mercy and washes
our sin.

~ Max Lucado

We've spent the last three days reading stories of, for all intents and purposes, forgiving the unforgiveable.

I'm curious . . . how have these stories affected you? Were you touched? Shocked? Inspired? If faced with the same situation, could you forgive in the same way?

Today we're going to address some hard stuff. I pray the things we'll talk about today haven't touched too many of your lives. But statistics show they have affected most of us in one way or another.

Pause for a moment and think of one situation that's happened in your life, or the life of a loved one, that you could never forgive. Ever. Forgiving the act is absolutely out of the question in your mind.

And if you haven't had to experience an unforgiveable act, I challenge you to think about and name one situation you would never be willing to forgive.

What would that be?

Addictions
Abuse
Adultery
Murder
Drunk driver
Rape

Are these crimes unforgiveable? In our human flesh, absolutely. Through Christ? No, nothing is impossible through Christ {Luke 1:37}.

How then, do we even begin to forgive these seemingly unforgiveable acts? My answer is simple—the same way we forgive smaller acts requiring forgiveness. As a start to forgiving, and ultimately healing process, here's a quick recap of what we've covered so far:

- We've been commanded to forgive.
- Jesus died a horrific death so we could live forgiven.
- Forgiveness is an act of grace.
- Forgiveness comes from love.
- Forgiveness brings freedom.
- Forgiveness is a choice.

Does this make it easy? Or something that'll happen over night? Absolutely not.

But I'm praying it gives a road map to understanding how and why. And that we let it soak deep into our hearts . . . that we soften our hearts to the process of forgiveness . . . that we let go of any bitterness and anger . . . that we make the choice to forgive and grab hold of the freedom it brings.

As you're trying to process and understand how to forgive something seemingly unforgiveable, think of Brian Banks, the man who spent five years in jail, and another five labeled and living as a sex offender—all for a crime he was innocent of. He understands hanging onto unforgiveness will hurt no one but himself.

And Ronald Cotton, who spent more than ten years in prison for raping Jennifer Thompson—a crime he never committed. Yet he forgives.

And Rebecca Nicols, who as a young child faced terror and loss that would change her life forever. She understands her need to, "Love and forgive others as {she's} been loved and forgiven by Jesus."

So. Now it's our turn. When faced with something seemingly unforgiveable, can we extend the same love, grace, and forgiveness as these examples? Examples nothing short of shining the very image of Jesus?

Over the next two days, I'll share more insight on forgiving the unforgiveable. We'll talk about forgiveness vs. condoning and enabling, and I'll share an important lesson I learned the hard way!

####

Friends, I'd like to make it very clear, if you're in any sort of on-going abusive situation, it's imperative you protect yourselves right away. Forgiving someone doesn't mean you allow abusive behavior to continue.

What If I Don't Forgive?
{day thirteen }

I firmly believe a great many prayers are not answered

because we are not willing to forgive someone.

~ *D.L. Moody*

One life-changing lesson I've learned, the hard way I might add, is to stay out of the way of God working in someone's life. It took me a few times—when the same situation occurred time and again—to truly forgive. When the situation first happened, I *said* I forgave, but when the situation happened again, I realized my forgiveness was far from a heart decision.

Through a lot of praying to, leaning on, and trusting in God, true forgiveness finally came into my heart. It was only then that I was able to see God's heavenly work begin.

When we harbor unforgiveness, we end up being barriers to God's work. We try to control situations the way we think they should go, and in the process interrupt any heavenly healing that might need to take place.

Why did it take me so long to finally get it? Quite honestly, I didn't want that person to think what he'd done was okay. And if I forgave and moved on like nothing happened, certainly I'd be condoning the behavior.

What I didn't understand at the time is forgiveness is for me. Forgiveness freed *me* from bitterness and anger. And ultimately, allowed God to work in the situation.

If we allow God to work in our situations, redemption is possible. I'd go so far as to say it's not just possible . . . but probable.

Of course each of our situations is very different. It's quite possible the person you're faced with doesn't want help and doesn't want to change. That's going to be an individual decision based on your unique situation.

You know the saying, "Are you sorry you got caught? Or are you sorry for what you've done?"

The following verse has been pivotal in my own life and experiences:

For the kind of sorrow God wants us to experience

leads us away from sin and results in salvation.

There's no regret for that kind of sorrow.

But worldly sorrow, which lacks repentance,

results in spiritual death.

2 Corinthians 7:10 {NLT}

If you're confused or wondering if someone has truly changed, I encourage you to pray and meditate over the above verse.

Don't hear me wrong though, regardless of the condition of someone's heart, we are still required to forgive. If someone isn't showing true repentance, it's not our place to judge or condemn—we're still required to forgive.

Lord, help us to realize You desire to work all things for our good. Help us to hand our situations over to You and step aside, trusting You to work. Father, we pray for godly repentance leading to redemption.

But Lord if it's not in Your great plan, we pray for peace and faith knowing You are at work. Thank you Father for Your promises.

Is Forgiving Condoning or Enabling?
{day fourteen }

Forgiveness does not mean excusing.

~ C. S. Lewis

It's important to understand condoning and/or enabling are not forgiving. We can forgive someone and not enable a behavior to continue.

Let's say we're in a situation where there's adultery, abuse, or addictions involved. How do we forgive without enabling the behavior?

It starts by going back to the core truths of forgiveness and the things we've covered. 1) God has commanded we forgive. 2) Forgiveness frees us, not the transgressor. 3) Forgiveness is rooted in grace—giving someone something she doesn't deserve. 4) Forgiveness allows God to move.

It is possible to forgive and not condone or enable a behavior. If one of the above behaviors involves you or someone in your life, it's important to seek godly counsel and wisdom. If it's an abusive situation, the abuser needs to get help and the victim needs to get out of harm's way immediately. An addict needs rehab and on-going counseling and AA meetings. And an adulterer needs counseling and possibly rehab or SA {sexual addiction} meetings.

Just because we've decided to forgive someone doesn't mean we allow the behavior to continue. In fact, it's very important we do all we can to help the person stop his/her destructive behavior.

I realize every situation is uniquely different, which is why it's so important to find someone we trust who can pray with us and give godly counsel.

This is a difficult subject matter and I'm not a counselor. I'm speaking only from my own experiences and what I believe to be true. As I've said, every situation is different and everyone reacts differently—both the person in need of forgiveness and the person forgiving.

And it's important to remember no matter the situation or temperature of the transgressor's heart, we're still required to forgive.

In his book, *Total Forgiveness,* author R.T. Kendall says, "Can a person totally forgive and yet at the same time be the one who reports the crime? Absolutely."

> *Your love must be real. Hate what is evil, and*
> *hold on to what is good.*
>
> *Romans 12:9 {NCV}*

"Love the sinner, hate the sin."

We need to check the temperature of our own hearts. Are we being vindictive or hateful, wanting them to "get what they deserve?"

True – a crime needs to be reported.

Equally true – we're required to extend forgiveness regardless of the situation.

Father, I pray for discernment for anyone reading these words. In light of difficult circumstances they may be faced with, I pray they're able to come to a place of true forgiveness—releasing any vengeance or hate. I pray Lord for real love in our hearts. A love found only in You. A love through which we can find true forgiveness.

If I Forgive, Am I
A Doormat?
{day fifteen}

Dear Lord, please show me everything I need to

understand about forgiveness and surrender.

~ *Elizabeth Gilbert*

The act of forgiveness doesn't mean we're saying, "What you've done is okay."

In fact, what's been done is most certainly not okay.

But it's so very, very important to remember, forgiveness is giving *ourselves* freedom from anger and bitterness. Forgiveness is a gift we give *ourselves*. It's not about what somebody did to us.

Often times we think if we forgive someone, we're letting him or her "get away with it." When we begin to understand that true forgiveness isn't about the other person, it's about us and the control we have over our own thoughts, actions, and life's path, then we begin to understand it's not about someone getting away with something.

And just because we extend forgiveness to someone, it doesn't mean we should be a doormat. Proverbs 4:23 says, "Guard your heart above all else, for it determines the course of your life."

If we're being hurt over and over, it's important we guard our own hearts, minds, and lives so we aren't entering into sin ourselves, be it with anger, bitterness, resentment, gossip, or unforgiveness.

With the right motives—meaning our hearts and intentions are pure—it's very important we guard ourselves.

So if, in order to protect our hearts, we need to politely decline coffee or lunch, and lessen our interaction with that person, then I think it's important to do so.

And let's not forget this era of social media we're in and how it can bring "ugly" to a whole new level. If it's out of anger or resentment we're moving toward removing someone from our lives, then we have the wrong motive. But if we've prayerfully checked our motives and know our hearts are pure, then if unfollowing someone on social media is going to guard our hearts and mind, I think it's okay to do it.

I was in a situation recently that caused me a lot of pain. I didn't want to unfollow the person causing the hurt—I didn't want to be *that* person. But every time I saw a post or photo, it would deepen my pain. I prayed about it and sought the advice of a godly woman I trust and she confirmed—if it's with the right motive and a pure heart, it's important to protect our own hearts, minds, and lives.

The honest truth is, when I would see something that caused me to feel hurt, it would cause ungodly thoughts and feelings in me. Basically causing me to sin. When that happens, it's important to remove ourselves from those situations.

Just because we forgive doesn't mean we let ourselves continue to be hurt. Everyone's situations are different and it's up to us to make sure we're living with godly intent and pure hearts.

Jesus, Friend of Sinners
{day sixteen}

Christ can take the most sin-laden, selfish, evil
person
and bring forgiveness and new life.

~ Billy Graham

It's no secret Jesus was a friend to sinners. He was most comfortable with the "least of these."

From birth, He was numbered with the transgressors. Mary and Joseph were coming to Bethlehem to register their names. A census was being taken and each person had to go to his or her capital city to register. Jesus was numbered with sinners.

The fact that Jesus was circumcised numbers Him with sinners. Circumcision was a rite administered admitting that one was a sinner. Clipping the extra skin signified the Hebrew shouldn't have sin in his life—we should be circumcised from sin. Jesus was circumcised signifying He identified with us. Jesus, a friend of sinners.

In Luke 5:27-29 we read the account of Matthew, a tax collector, and his decision to follow Jesus Christ. A tax collector wasn't thought highly of in that day. They were classified as greedy, often taking more money than they were entitled to.

Excited about his decision, Matthew hosted a banquet in his home, inviting all the publicans and sinners together. Among this motley crew, Jesus was the guest of honor. Jesus, a friend of sinners.

In John chapter 4, we read of Jesus and an adulterous Samaritan woman at a well. Jesus knew she had five husbands, yet living with a man who wasn't her husband. Still, Jesus sat at the well with her, not to condemn or judge her, but to minister to and encourage her. Jesus, a friend of sinners.

Jesus was a friend to blind Bartimaeus beside the road, to Nicodemus at midnight, and Zacchaeus, with whom He shared a meal. Jesus, a friend of sinners.

In His last dying breaths on the cross, Jesus saved a thief saying, "I assure you, today you will be with me in paradise." {Luke 23:43, NLT} Jesus, a friend of sinners.

> *The Son of Man came eating and drinking, and*
> *you say,*
> *"Look at him! He eats too much and drinks too*
> *much wine,*
> *and he is a friend of tax collectors and sinners!"*
> *Luke 7:34 {NCV}*

I say praise God that Jesus is a friend of sinners. Praise God He eats with sinners. Praise God He sits and communes with sinners. Praise God He said, "Healthy people don't need a doctor—sick people do. I have come to call not those who think they are righteous, but those who know they are sinners." {Mark 2:17 NLT}

Friends, we are all sinners. We have all fallen short of the glory of God.

All of us.

One of us is no better than the next.

Can we too, come along side the broken-hearted, the needy, and the fallen? Not with judgment and condemnation, but with love and grace?

Following in the footsteps of our Savior, shouldn't we too, be a friend of sinners?

"Jesus, Friend of Sinners"

Written by Matthew West and Mark Hall

:: Performed by Casting Crowns ::

Jesus friend of sinners we have strayed so far away

We cut down people in your name but the sword was never ours to swing

Jesus friend of sinners the truth's become so hard to see

The world is on their way to You but they're tripping over me

Always looking around but never looking up I'm so double minded

A plank eyed saint with dirty hands and a heart divided

{chorus}

Oh Jesus friend of sinners

Open our eyes to world at the end of our pointing fingers

Let our hearts be led by mercy

Help us reach with open hearts and open doors

Oh Jesus friend of sinners break our hearts for what breaks yours

Jesus friend of sinners the one who's writing in the sand

Make the righteous turn away and the stones fall from their hands

Help us to remember we are all the least of these

Let the memory of Your mercy bring your people to their knees

Nobody knows what we're for only against when we judge the wounded

What if we put down our signs crossed over the lines and loved like You did

{chorus}

You love every lost cause; you reach for the outcast

For the leper and the lame; they're the reason that You came

Lord I was that lost cause and I was the outcast

But you died for sinners just like me a grateful leper at Your feet

'Cause You are good, You are good And Your love endures forever

You are good, You are good and Your love endures forever

You are good, You are good and Your love endures forever

You are good, You are good and Your love endures forever

{chorus}

And I was the lost cause and I was the outcast

You died for sinners just like me, a grateful leper at Your feet

Forgive and Forget?
{day seventeen}

I can forgive, but I cannot forget, is only another
way of saying,

I will not forgive. Forgiveness ought to be like a
cancelled note—torn in two, and

burned up, so that it never can be shown against
one.

~ *Henry Ward Beecher*

While watching a recent episode of a certain reality show I indulge in, an all-out war was raged between two best friends. Friend #1 made the only choice she thought she had, and it hurt the feelings of friend #2.

Friend #2 could not, and did not, try to understand why friend #1 made the choice she did. Instead she became angry and declared, "She is dead to me!" In another episode friend #2 declared, "I forgive friend #1, but I will NEVER forget what she did."

And there we have it. Is it really possible to forgive and forget? Are we required to forgive and forget? If we don't forget, is it really forgiveness? Does God forgive and forget?

Let's start there. Does God forgive and forget?

The Bible tells us God is omniscient, which means He is all-knowing. So if He's all-knowing, that tells us He knows all and remembers all.

What then of this Scripture?

And I will forgive their wickedness,

and I will never again remember their sins.

Hebrews 8:12 {NLT}

Of course He still remembers, He's omniscient. And of course we still remember, we're human. But I think it goes back to our heart-motive. And remember, forgiveness comes from love. So to say to someone {in anger}, "I forgive you. But I will never forget what you did," doesn't sound too loving . . . or forgiving. And it also sounds like the offense just might be brought up a time or two.

Here's the thing with God . . . and a lesson that serves us well. God chooses NOT to remember our sins. He chooses NOT to bring them up ever again.

In the verse above, ". . . and I will never again remember their sins," the word "remember" means this in the original Greek language:

mimnéskó: properly recall, bring to mind, remind oneself actively (purposefully); to remember, have in mind, "be mindful of."

And the GOD'S WORD translation translates the verse this way:

. . . because I will forgive their wickedness and

I will no longer hold their sins against them.

Hebrews 8:12 {GOD'S WORD}

This, my friends, is the way we should "forgive and forget." This is what happens when our forgiveness comes from a place of love. We no longer hold the offense against someone. We don't actively remind ourselves, recall, or purposefully remember the offense.

76

And when we're not actively allowing that offense to come into our minds and hearts, it's much easier to let go of the hurt, anger, and bitterness. Which then makes it much easier to move on to a place of freedom in our lives.

Is Forgiveness an Option?
{day eighteen}

Not forgiving is like drinking rat poison and
then waiting for the rat to die.

~ *Anne Lamott*

What are your thoughts? Do you think forgiveness is an option? Based on what we've learned so far and based on what we've been told in Matthew 6:14-15 {NLT}:

If you forgive those who sin against you, your heavenly

Father will forgive you. But if you refuse to forgive others,

your Father will not forgive your sins.

I'd say no, forgiveness isn't an option.

Well . . . actually, let me take that back. I suppose forgiveness is an option if we:

- Don't want God to forgive our sins and live forgiven
- Want to live bound in shackles of bitterness, resentment, and pain
- Don't want to live in freedom

- Don't want to show Christ's love to others
- Want to live physically unhealthy from symptoms of unforgiveness

Just to name a few. I think we get the idea!

Friends, when we're leashed up to anger, unforgiveness, and resentment . . . do you realize what we're dragging around through life with us? Here's a story that illustrates this point well:

It's a beautiful day so we decide to spend some time at the local park. While we're there, we find a bench in a lovely area and sit for a while. But we soon discover we're not alone on this bench. Instead, our constant companions unforgiveness, anger, bitterness, resentment, and pain have decided to join us. A while later, when we get up to walk away, we realize all that junk is still with us. It's tied up to the bench, and tied up to us and if we won't release it from our lives, it's like literally dragging a park bench of ugly emotions through life. Exhausting.

Forgiveness is the gift of freedom. Forgiveness is the ultimate gift that money cannot buy.

For **give** ness.

But back to the original question . . . is forgiveness an option? I suppose it is. After all, we've been given free will.

Maybe a better question is, "Do we really want to live a life *burdened* by unforgiveness?"

Forgiveness Is An Act of the Will
{day nineteen}

Forgiveness is an act of the will,

and the will can function regardless of

the temperature of the heart.

~ Corrie Ten Boom

Have you heard the saying, "Love isn't a feeling, it's a choice"? Let's take a minute to explore that statement.

When we love someone based on feelings, most often we're let down and disappointed. That's the stuff divorce is made of. I can make a liberal statement like that because I've been there. I know.

I didn't *feel* happy. I didn't *feel* my needs weren't being met. So I made the choice to leave . . . based on my feelings.

We are a fallen people, living in a fallen world. We are going to be let down and disappointed. And if we act on every feeling and emotion we have, we're going to continue to be disappointed.

In my second marriage, as I grew closer to the Lord and understood what real love {through Christ} is all about, I made the choice not to leave. Was I let down and disappointed during my marriage? Oh you bet! Too many times to count! And if I was living out that marriage based on feelings, I'd-a-been long gone!

But I made a choice to love.

If we understand forgiveness comes from love, and love comes from God, then we can begin to understand if we're rooted deeply in Christ, we can choose to love. And ultimately to forgive.

We can't, and shouldn't, base forgiveness on an emotion. In our human minds and strength, most often, we don't want to forgive.

We've been wronged. The person doesn't deserve forgiveness. End of story.

I love the quote above from Corrie Ten Boom . . . regardless of what's going on in your heart, be it anger, hurt, resentment, bitterness . . . you can choose to forgive. It's an act of the will.

Do everything in love.

1 Corinthians 16:14 {NIV}

Three Strikes, You're out?
{day twenty}

Then Peter came to him and asked, "Lord, how often
should I forgive someone who sins against me?
Seven times?"

Matthew 18:21 {NLT}

Back in the day . . . like way back in the day when Jesus was on earth, rabbis taught if you forgave someone three times for an offense, it was like huge I-should-be-a-saint forgiveness! So when Peter came to Jesus and asked how often he should forgive someone, "Seven times?" He thought Jesus would crown him the saint of forgiveness right there on the spot. Forgiving seven times would be EPIC and people would be sure to talk about it for years to come.

Talk about it for years to come, indeed. But not quite the way Peter thought.

"No, not seven times," Jesus replied, "but seventy times seven!"

That's 490 times, my friends. And not that we're supposed to literally keep count—it's an arbitrarily large number meaning we forgive and forgive and forgive.

In Luke 17:4 Jesus told His disciples, "If he sins against you seven times in a day, and seven times comes back to you and says, 'I repent,' forgive him."

Forgiving the *same person* seven times in one day seems ludicrous! How in the world can we be expected to forgive someone who repeatedly offends us . . . in one day's time no less?

Friends, to put it bluntly, we do it because we've been commanded to do it. We do it because we live forgiven.

When we come before God and ask forgiveness, He doesn't go into our past offenses and say, "Um, you were here just ten minutes ago asking forgiveness. Sorry, your quota's up!"

Can you imagine? My word, I sure am thankful I can live forgiven again, and again, and again. Without a laundry list of each sin I've already been forgiven for.

So how many times do we forgive? I suppose we could ask ourselves, how many times do we want to be forgiven? Sometimes I need all seventy times seven in one day!

Lord, help me to always . . . in everything I do, in every thought I have . . . give to others what You've so graciously given to me.

Give unto Others
{day twenty-one}

Whenever I see myself before God and realize something

of what my blessed Lord has done for me at Calvary,

I am ready to forgive anybody anything. I cannot withhold it.

I do not even want to withhold it.

~ Martyn Lloyd-Jones

Continuing from yesterday's message, Matthew 18:23-35, the following is a parable Jesus shared with His disciples:

> "The kingdom of God is like a king who decided to square accounts with his servants. As he got under way, one servant was brought before him who had run up a debt of a hundred thousand dollars. He couldn't pay up, so the king ordered the man, along with his wife, children, and goods, to be auctioned off at the slave market.
>
> The poor wretch threw himself at the king's feet and begged, 'Give me a chance and I'll pay it all back.' Touched by his plea, the king let him off, erasing the debt.
>
> The servant was no sooner out of the room when

*he came upon one of his fellow servants who owed
him ten dollars. He seized him by the throat and
demanded, 'Pay up. Now!'*

*The poor wretch threw himself down and begged,
'Give me a chance and I'll pay it all back.' But
he wouldn't do it. He had him arrested and put
in jail until the debt was paid. When the other
servants saw this going on, they were outraged
and brought a detailed report to the king.*

*The king summoned the man and said, 'You evil
servant! I forgave your entire debt when you
begged me for mercy. Shouldn't you be compelled to
be merciful to your fellow servant who asked for
mercy?' The king was furious and put the screws
to the man until he paid back his entire debt.
And that's exactly what my Father in heaven is
going to do to each one of you who doesn't forgive
unconditionally anyone who asks for mercy."*

If we know and have been shown God's mercy, we must operate on the principle of mercy. We must.

So you must show mercy to others, or God will not

show mercy to you when he judges you.

But the person who shows mercy can stand

without fear at the judgment.

James 2:13 {NCV}

An even better ending to that verse comes from the New International Version – "Mercy triumphs over judgment!"

Mercy = compassion or forgiveness shown toward someone whom it is within one's power to punish or harm.

Judgment = form an opinion or conclusion about

You have the ability to punish someone based on your opinion, or based on evidence. The master had the bills/receipts/facts showing the servant owed him a lot of money. But the master had mercy on him and let him go.

Moments later—mere moments, mind you—the servant was then faced with the exact same situation, only this time the debt was for ten dollars, not one hundred thousand! Yet the selfish servant insisted the debt be paid. And when it couldn't, he had the debtor thrown into jail.

How often are we guilty of the same? We come before the throne asking forgiveness and mercy. God grants it to us allowing us to walk away unburdened, with a clean slate.

Only to turn around and throw our fellow neighbors into jail because we can't give what's just been given to us.

Hypocritical, no?

Lord, thank you for your unending mercy and love. Help me Lord to walk in Your image everyday and in everything I do. Lord, my desire is to be a reflection of Your great love. Father, give me Your heart to love others as You love them. Help me to see them through eyes of mercy, grace, and love—in the same way you look at me.

Forgiving Oneself
{day twenty-two}

Forgiveness is always free. But that doesn't mean that

confession is always easy. Sometimes it is hard.

Incredibly hard. It is painful to admit our sins

and entrust ourselves to God's care.

~ Erwin Lutzer

Why is it we have such a hard time forgiving ourselves? There are many feelings we may be burying deep in our hearts keeping us from living in freedom—anger, shame, guilt, blame—just to name a few, not allowing us full healing and forgiveness.

Or, quite possibly, the situation might be that we've done something requiring forgiveness from someone else, but that person is withholding it from us.

If that's the case, I urge you to remember everything we've learned about forgiveness thus far. These facts are equally important to remember when it comes to forgiving ourselves.

- *We've been commanded to forgive {and yes, this means ourselves too}*
- *Forgiveness gives us freedom*
- *Forgiveness allows God to move {in our lives too!}*
- *Forgiveness is rooted in grace {giving us something we don't deserve}*

Not forgiving ourselves is just as wrong as not forgiving others. God loves you and desires for you to live free and forgiven as much as He desires it for your neighbor.

There are many, many things I have done in my life against God, against myself, and against others. I could hate myself for some of the destructive things I've done. But to live in the past wouldn't do me, or anyone in my life, any good.

I've repented of the things I've done, and I know I stand forgiven . . . by the One who matters most.

> *But if we confess our sins, he will forgive our sins,*
>
> *because we can trust God to do what is right.*
>
> *He will cleanse us from all the wrongs we have done.*
>
> *1 John 1:9 {NCV}*

I've been in situations where forgiveness has been withheld from me. And I've come to understand it's their choice. But just because they choose to live in a prison of unforgiveness doesn't mean I have to sit in there with them.

Another perspective comes from R.T. Kendall in his book, *Total Forgiveness*, "Forgiving yourself may bring about the breakthrough you have been looking for. It could set you free in ways you have never experienced before."

The things we've been through, even if they are shameful or destructive, could very well be things God wants to use in our lives to help others. And if we're standing in the way of our forgiveness, healing, and freedom, how can God do His work in our lives?

Wouldn't we rather have God bring glory to those undesirable seasons in our lives?

And friends—we'll touch on this further tomorrow, but ultimately, if God forgives us, how can we not forgive ourselves?

He's the final judge and it's under His standards we should live. So if His Word promises we can live forgiven, why wouldn't we?

Does God Really Forgive?
{day twenty-three}

*". . . as far as sunrise is from sunset, he has
separated us from our sins."*

Psalm 103:12 {MSG}

In working on this series, I put out a couple of requests asking people for their questions and concerns relating to forgiveness. Here's one comment I received and I feel it's in the hearts of many others:

*I struggle with wondering if *I* am really forgiven (by God) or is He going to punish me for something I've asked for forgiveness for?*

Does anyone else struggle with these thoughts?

The first thing we need to realize is God knows all. Whether you ask Him for forgiveness or not . . . whether you *admit* it to Him or not . . . He already knows what you need to confess.

In 1 Chronicles 28:9, the Bible tells us He knows not only our actions, He knows our thoughts, and He even knows our hearts. Meaning, even if something doesn't make it into our thoughts and played out in our actions, He already knows our heart-motives . . . that which is hidden deep down in there.

Nothing in all the world can be hidden from God.
Everything is clear and lies open before him,

and to him we must explain the way we have
lived.

Hebrews 4:13 {NCV}

Which is why a frequent prayer has me asking God to purify my heart and bring to mind any ugly that might be hiding in there.

Search me, O God, and know my heart;

test me and know my anxious thoughts.

Point out anything in me that offends you,

and lead me along the path of everlasting life.

Psalm 139:23-24 {NCV}

Secondly, the Bible tells us God doesn't punish us for sin. If we are believers in Christ Jesus and have repented of our sin, it's gone. Our sins have been nailed on the cross with Jesus.

He does not punish us for all our sins;

he does not deal harshly with us, as we deserve.

Psalm 103:10 {NLT}

However . . . and if you'll indulge me some wordiness here . . . there is a difference between punishment and discipline.

Discipline is derived from the word "disciple." To train or instruct.

If sin continually remains in our lives and we don't repent and turn from that sin, God may require His divine discipline. If He didn't, He wouldn't be a loving and concerned Father.

The Bible tells us in Hebrews 12:4-11 {MSG}:

In this all-out match against sin, others have
suffered far worse than you, to say nothing of
what

Jesus went through—all that bloodshed! So don't
feel sorry for yourselves. Or have you forgotten
how good parents treat children, and that God
regards you as his children?

My dear child, don't shrug off God's discipline,
but don't be crushed by it either.
It's the child he loves that he disciplines;
the child he embraces, he also corrects.

God is educating you; that's why you must never
drop out. He's treating you as dear children.

This trouble you're in isn't punishment; it's
training, the normal experience of children. Only

irresponsible parents leave children to fend for
themselves. Would you prefer an irresponsible

God? We respect our own parents for training and
not spoiling us, so why not embrace God's

training so we can truly live? While we were
children, our parents did what seemed best to

them. But God is doing what is best for us,
training us to live God's holy best. At the time,

discipline isn't much fun. It always feels like it's
going against the grain. Later, of course, it pays

off handsomely, for it's the well-trained who find
themselves mature in their relationship

with God.

All that to say . . . if you're living a life of repeated sin and could care less what God thinks about it, you may find yourself under His discipline.

On the other hand, if you have asked for God's forgiveness and are truly sorry for something you've done, Psalm 103:12 {MSG} says, ". . . as far as sunrise is from sunset, he has separated us from our sins."

And don't forget the verse we talked about a few days ago:

For the kind of sorrow God wants us to experience

leads us away from sin and results in salvation.

There's no regret for that kind of sorrow.

But worldly sorrow, which lacks repentance,

results in spiritual death.

2 Corinthians 7:10 {NLT}

The Bible tells us story after story after story of God's love and redemption. Many a prophet, king, and disciple sinned against God, yet as soon as they repented, God provided restoration in their lives.

The same is true for us today.

God loves us. With an unconditional, unending, unfathomable love. Nothing can *ever* separate us from God's love.

But in all these things we are completely victorious

through God who showed his love for us. Yes, I am

sure that neither death, nor life, nor angels, nor

ruling spirits, nothing now, nothing in the future,

no powers, nothing above us, nothing below us,

nor anything else in the whole world will ever be

able to separate us from the love of God that is in

Christ Jesus our Lord.

Romans 8:37–39 {NCV}

Does God really forgive us? Yes. Yes. Yes. Yes. And . . . YES!

And not only does He forgive us . . . it's His desire to forgive us. He sent His very own Son to die so we could be forgiven, so we could live a forgiven life.

Thank you Father for your great love, sacrifice, and forgiveness. All of which we don't deserve, yet through Your wondrous mercy and grace you make available to each of us . . . the least of these.

The Veil Was Torn
{day twenty-four}

Before the foundation of the world was laid, God,

in His divine sovereignty, planned to send His

own Son to the cross to be our Savior.

~ Anne Graham Lotz

Why did Jesus die on the cross? The short and simple answer is . . . so we could be forgiven of our sins and have eternal life in heaven.

Today may be a tad off topic and a bit in-depth, but I've been asked the question, and I find the answer so awesome. AWEsome, in every sense of the word. Case-in-point, I was just moved to tears as I was diving deeper into the Word and new revelations on the power of forgiveness touched me.

Starting at the very beginning . . . God created humans and the earth to be perfect. But ever since Adam and Eve disobeyed God in the garden of Eden, a time also known as "the fall of man," we've been born into sin.

> *You know the story of how Adam landed us in*
> *the dilemma we're in—first sin, then death, and*
> *no one exempt from either sin or death. That*
> *sin disturbed relations with God in everything*
> *and everyone, but the extent of the disturbance*
> *was not clear until God spelled it out in detail*
> *to Moses. So death, this huge abyss separating us*

from God, dominated the landscape from Adam
to Moses. Even those who didn't sin precisely as
Adam did by disobeying a specific command of
God still had to experience this termination of life,
this separation from God. But Adam, who got us
into this, also points ahead to the One who will
get us out of it.

Romans 5:12-14 {MSG}

Whew! Follow that?

You see, because God is infinitely holy and righteous, overlooking sin would make Him unjust. The punishment for sin is death {a separation from God}. In Romans 6:23 we read, "For the wages of sin is death, but the free gift of God is eternal life through Christ Jesus our Lord."

Because one person disobeyed God, many became
sinners.

But because one other person obeyed God, many will be
made righteous.

Romans 5:19 {NLT}

But our loving God didn't leave us without hope. He promised to send a Sacrifice to take the punishment we deserved. Until that day, men would sacrifice innocent animals, showing their repentance of sins and faith in God's promise of a future Sacrifice. God declared without the shedding of blood, there is no forgiveness {Hebrews 9:22}.

And because God is the only one who's sinless, the sacrifice would have to be sinless and without blemish, which is why Jesus {God made flesh} had to die on the cross.

So that man was no longer required to offer animals as sacrifice for our sins, Jesus came as the ultimate Sacrifice so we could live forgiven and have eternal life with God in heaven.

I'd like to close by sharing something I find incredibly moving and beautiful. In the Old Testament {the old covenant}, 1 Kings 6, we read of Solomon building the first temple of the Lord.

The temple contained two rooms. The first room, an outer room was called the Holy Place. Throughout the year, priests would regularly enter this outer room to carry out their ministry and worship.

The second room, an inner room was called the Most Holy Place or the Holy of Holies. The Holy of Holies was separated from the rest of the temple by a veil and was the earthly dwelling place of God's presence. The veil signified man's separation from God by sin and only the high priest was allowed to pass beyond the veil once a year. Each year the high priest would enter into God's presence with a sacrifice to make atonement for himself and the sins of the people.

Based on the writings of first century Jewish historian Josephus, the veil between the two rooms is believed to be somewhere near 60 feet high and four inches thick—so thick that horses tied to each side couldn't pull the veil apart.

Then Jesus shouted out again, and he released his spirit.

At that moment the curtain in the sanctuary of the

Temple was torn in two, from top to bottom.

The earth shook, rocks split apart.

Matthew 27:50-51 {emphasis mine}

When Jesus, the new covenant Sacrifice, died, the veil was torn in two, from top to bottom signifying we now have full access to God.

The veil is symbolic of Christ as the only way to the Father. Under the old covenant, the high priest had to pass through the veil to enter the presence of God. Christ is now our High Priest and we can enter into God's presence through Him {John 14:6}.

> So, friends, we can now—without hesitation—
> walk right up to God,
>
> into "the Holy Place." Jesus has cleared the way by
> the blood of his sacrifice,
>
> acting as our priest before God. The "curtain" into
> God's presence is his body.
>
> Hebrews 10:19-20 {MSG}

I'm in complete awe of the detail in each event and prophecy . . . all so we could live free and forgiven lives! God planned this out in the most intricate of detail and it strikes me again and again . . . if God went to this much "trouble" for us, how can we not find it within ourselves to forgive our fellow sinners?

If you'd like to do some reading for yourselves, I encourage you to read through some of the following Scriptures:

Exodus 30:10
Leviticus 16
Hebrews 9 & 10

Doers of the Word
{day twenty-five}

Christians are the most forgiven people in the world.

Therefore, we should be the most forgiving people in the world.

~ Ken Sande

That quote says it all! And after all this writing, I kinda wanna yell at y'all . . . "For the love of God people, can't we all just love each other and get along!?"

But let's pretend I didn't write that and it's just me thinking aloud . . . kind of.

The Bible tells us over and over again to love each other {as Christ loves us}, to forgive each other {as Christ forgives us}, to be imitators of Christ, and be doers of the Word.

> *But don't just listen to God's word. You must do what it says. Otherwise, you are only fooling yourselves. For if you listen to the word and don't obey, it is like glancing at your face in a mirror. You see yourself, walk away, and forget what you look like. But if you look carefully into the perfect law that sets you free, and if you do what it says and don't forget what you heard, then God will bless you for doing it.*
>
> *James 1:22-25 {NLT}*

Sometimes Christians can be the biggest hypocrites of us all. My husband, who is new in his faith, has said many times, both before and after receiving God, "That doesn't seem very 'Christian.'"

True. We are all sinners and we all slip up. Those momentary slips aren't the things I'm speaking of. I'm speaking of someone who claims to be a Christian, yet lives in such a way that Jesus isn't shining through his/her everyday life.

Get rid of all bitterness, rage, anger, harsh words,
and slander, as well as all types of evil behavior.
Ephesians 4:31 {NLT}

Instead, be kind to each other, tenderhearted,
forgiving one another, just as God through Christ
has forgiven you.
Ephesians 4:32 {NLT}

Imitate God, therefore, in everything you do,
because you are
his dear children. Live a life filled with love,
following the example of Christ.
Ephesians 5:1-2a {NLT}

According to the above Scriptures, we can break it down this way:

- Get rid of all the ugly inside of us {remember, it's our choice . . . do we choose to keep the ugly, or do we choose to live in freedom?}.

- Be kind, tenderhearted, forgiving . . . just as God has forgiven us.

- How do we do this? Imitate God and follow His example.

Lord, help me to release any ugly thoughts that may be buried in my heart. It's my desire to live in the freedom You have available to me. Lord, keep me tenderhearted, kind, and forgiving toward everyone I encounter. Help me Lord to follow your example and imitate you in everything I do.

Bless Those Who Curse You
{day twenty-six}

Forgiveness is the well from which we draw

the water to wash others' feet.

~ D. Siler

I'm going to address two important issues today: pursuing resolution, and blessing those who curse us.

Pursuing Resolution

We are called to live vertical lives looking heavenward, not horizontally—looking at what our neighbors are doing. "She's mad at me; she started it; I'll forgive when she apologizes first." Unforgiveness blocks the flow between heaven and us.

In Matthew 5:21-26 we read about anger, unforgiveness, and unresolved conflict.

In verses 21 and 22, we're warned against anger. The Bible says, "Anyone who is so much as angry with a brother or sister is guilty of murder." It also warns:

> *Carelessly call a brother 'idiot!' and you just might*
> *find yourself hauled into court. Thoughtlessly yell*
> *'stupid!' at a sister and you are on the brink of*
> *hellfire. The simple moral fact is that words kill.*

Matthew 5:22 {MSG}

Verses 23 through 26 speak of reconciliation. As we've discussed previously, reconciliation isn't always possible, God knows the situation and the temperature of your heart. He also knows when reconciliation is possible and should be attempted.

We should live with "short accounts" and work to resolve issues quickly, before bitterness and resentment grow in our hearts. Romans 12:18 says, "Do all that you can to live in peace with everyone." And Colossians 3:13, "Make allowance for each other's faults, and forgive anyone who offends you. Remember, the Lord forgave you, so you must forgive others."

In verse 26, Jesus tells us to settle matters quickly with our adversaries. We're directed to run *to* the problem, not *from* the problem. Whether we're right or wrong, it's our responsibility to pursue resolution.

I learned a lesson years ago, one that holds true today and one I try to instill in my children . . . never burn a bridge with someone. We never know when our paths may cross again or we may need that person some day.

Bless Those Who Curse Us

The world tells us it's okay to hate our enemies. But the Bible instructs we're to love our enemies.

> *"If you love only those who love you, why should you get*
> *credit for that? Even sinners love those who love them!*
> *And if you do good only to those who do good to you,*
> *why should you get credit? Even sinners do that much!*
> *And if you lend money only to those who can repay you*
> *why should you get credit? Even sinners will lend*
> *to other sinners for a full return."*
>
> *Luke 6:32-34 {NLT}*

*"I tell you, love your enemies. Help and give without expecting a return. **You'll never—I promise—regret it.** Live out this God-created identity the way our Father lives toward us, generously and graciously, even when we're at our worst. Our Father is kind; you be kind."*

Luke 6:35-36 {MSG, emphasis mine}

Anyone can love the loveable. But it takes a true Christ-follower to love and pray blessings over someone who hates you.

The Bible tells us countless times to love others . . . including our enemies.

"But to you who are willing to listen, I say, love your enemies!

Do good to those who hate you. Bless those who curse you.

Pray for those who hurt you."

Luke 6:27-28 {NLT}

In Romans 12 we're warned to "not be overcome by evil, but overcome evil with good." That's a hard thing to do sometimes. But when we're rooted in God's love and grace, it makes it a whole lot easier to extend it to others.

Love, grace, and forgiveness are the language of heaven. Which language are we speaking?

The Prodigal Son
:: Part 1 ::
{day twenty-seven}

Those who have served God for a long time and have been kept

from gross sins have a great deal to be humbly thankful for,

but nothing to proudly boast about.

~ Matthew Henry

There are so many great lessons in this one parable! Lessons on pride, greed, faith, hope, acceptance, repentance, and forgiveness.

I've spent {a few too many} hours studying Matthew Henry's commentary on the prodigal son and will be using quotes from *The New Matthew Henry Commentary* throughout the next couple days of writings.

Responding to the Pharisees mutterings that Jesus is a friend of sinners, outlined in Luke 15, Jesus shares with them three parables—one of a lost sheep, one of a lost coin, and one of a lost son.

Henry says, "The scope of all three parables is the same, namely, to show not only what God had said and sworn in the Old Testament, that he has no pleasure in the death and ruin of sinners, but also that he has great pleasure in their return and repentance."

My thoughts are running in twenty different directions right now, so I pray I'm able to bundle them together in a way that makes sense to someone other than myself!

First a quick summary of the prodigal son:

> A father has two sons—an elder who is the "good" son, and a younger who is the "bad" son. The younger son insisted his father give him his share of the estate, so the father divided the property, gave the younger son what was his, and the son took off.
>
> While away, the son "squandered his wealth with wild living." When he was left with nothing, a severe famine fell on the country, causing the boy to work in the fields feeding pigs. So hungry himself, he wanted to eat the swine's food, but was denied.
>
> After some time, he "came to his senses," and decided to go home. He planned to apologize to his father, saying, "Father, I have sinned against heaven and against you. I am no longer worthy to be called your son; make me like one of your hired men." And so he went to his father.
>
> His father, having faith knowing his son would return one day, saw his son while he was still a long way off. When his father saw his son, he was "filled with compassion for him; he ran to his son, threw his arms around him and kissed him." His father dressed him in the finest clothing and threw a lavish feast saying, "This son of mine was dead and is alive again; he was lost and is found."
>
> Unfortunately, the older son did not share in his father's joy. In fact, the Bible tells us he "became angry and refused to go into the party." The older son felt slighted

and tells his father, "All these years I've been slaving for you and never disobeyed your orders. Yet you never gave me even a young goat so I could celebrate with my friends. But when this son of yours who has squandered your property with prostitutes comes home, you kill the fattened calf for him!"

The father tenderly comes alongside his older son explaining, "But we had to celebrate and be glad, because this brother of yours was dead and is alive again; he was lost and is found."

We're going to spend the next two days in this story, and I probably could've written for another two days. As I mentioned, so many good lessons in this parable!

First up—let's address the issues of pride, greed, and idolatry. There's a difference in pride that stems from self-righteousness and the kind we feel for a job well done.

> *The wicked people are too proud. They do not look*
> *for God;*
>
> *there is no room for God in their thoughts.*
>
> *Psalm 10:4 {NCV}*

This kind of pride is opposite to the spirit of humility God wants us to walk in.

> *Pride leads to disgrace,*
>
> *but with humility comes wisdom.*
>
> *Proverbs 11:12 {NLT}*

Pride and greed are intertwined. I've heard they're two sides of the same coin. "Pride is taking pleasure in being ahead, greed is discontent over being behind."

And greed and idolatry are intertwined. A greedy person puts possessions at a higher priority than God.

Does that also mean pride is a form of idolatry? Well ... if we're putting ourselves on a list higher than God, then yes ... pride is a form of idolatry.

In his book, *Mere Christianity*, C.S. Lewis says, "Pride gets no pleasure out of having something, only out of having more of it than the next man. It is the comparison that makes you proud: the pleasure of being above the rest. Once the element of competition is gone, pride is gone."

Now back to our prodigal. Matthew Henry says, "He was proud of himself and had an inflated opinion of his own abilities. He thought that if only he had his share in his own hands now, he could manage it better than his father did and make better use of it. More young people are ruined by pride than by any other vice."

Another facet of pride is how it relates to forgiveness. Pride can keep people from *asking* for forgiveness, and it can also keep people from *offering* forgiveness.

Hold that thought. We'll be exploring those issues tomorrow!

Father, thank you for the lessons found in this parable. Lord, I pray we recognize a piece of ourselves throughout this story. Work in our hearts Lord and reveal to us where changes need to be made.

The Prodigal Son
:: Part 2 ::
{day twenty-eight}

*The circumstances of the parable set out the riches
of Gospel*

*grace much more fully, and to poor sinners ever
since it has been*

*indescribably useful, and so it will be as long as
the world exists.*

~ Matthew Henry

Yesterday we talked about pride, greed, and idolatry and how they're intertwined into forgiveness.

Today we'll discuss humility and repentance in light of forgiveness.

The opposite of pride is humility . . . and humility is required in forgiveness. When pride causes us to think of ourselves as righteous {we're right, they're wrong}, forgiveness will likely never come.

You know the saying, "what goes up must come down"? The book of Proverbs says it this way:

*Pride leads to destruction; a proud attitude brings
ruin.*

Proverbs 16:18 {NCV}

And that's exactly what our prodigal experienced. He squandered his inheritance, found himself feeding pigs, and was so hungry, "he longed to fill his stomach with the pods that the pigs were eating, but no one gave him anything."

At his lowest point, the bottom of the pride-totem pole, he "came to his senses" and thought of returning home. He fully didn't expect to enter back into the fold of his family. Instead, his greatest hope was to be hired by his father as a servant.

Matthew Henry says, "True repentance is rising and coming back to God."

> *For the kind of sorrow God wants us to experience*
>
> *leads us away from sin and results in salvation.*
>
> *There's no regret for that kind of sorrow.*
>
> *But worldly sorrow, which lacks repentance*
>
> *results in spiritual death.*
>
> *2 Corinthians 7:10 {NLT}*

Our prodigal humbly admitted to his father that he'd sinned. Both against heaven, and against his father . . . in that order.

On the other side of that equation we have the father. Luke 15:20 says, ". . . but while he was still a long way off, his father saw him and was fill with compassion for him; he ran to his son, threw his arms around him and kissed him."

His father was filled with expectation—faith—*knowing* his son would return home. His son was *a long way off*, but his father was waiting, watching, for him.

This prodigal had basically spit in his father's face. Greedily taking his share of the inheritance. Leaving the family for dead. Squandering every single penny. And then having the nerve to show his face back at the ranch!

Yet his father forgave him.

Without a moment's hesitation, he forgave his son.

As Henry said, "{With} great love and affection the father received the son. He expressed his kindness even before the son expressed his repentance."

He didn't expect his son to grovel and ask for forgiveness. The father had forgiveness buried in his heart.

"Not one word of rebuke," Henry notes.

True, pure-hearted, forgiveness keeps no record of wrongdoing.

The Prodigal Son
:: Part 3 ::
{day twenty-nine}

*Now this shows how we tend to make the worst of
everything*

*and to paint the picture in the darkest colors,
which is not doing*

*as we would have others do to us, nor as our
heavenly Father does to us.*

~ Matthew Henry

The prodigal son experienced true humility that led him back home and his father extended true forgiveness, but the story doesn't end "happily ever after" at that point.

Instead we have the elder brother. The good son. The one who Matthew Henry says, "represents those who are really good and never went astray, who—by comparison—need no repentance."

The elder son was out in the field when his father and brother reconciled. Luke 15:25 says, ". . . when he came near the house, he heard music and dancing." And he became angry and refused to go in {verse 28}.

"This shows us a common fault," Henry notes. And he has these two important points:

1. In people's families. Those who have always been a comfort to their parents think they should have a

monopoly of their parents' favors, and they tend to be too sharp toward those who have disobeyed.

2.   In God's family. Those who are comparatively innocent seldom know how to be compassionate toward those who are clearly penitents.

We read in Luke that the father went out to him and "pleaded with him." But he answered his father, "Look! All these years I've been slaving for you and never disobeyed your orders."

According to Henry, "It is too common for those who are better than their neighbors to boast about it." He goes on to say, "Those who have served God for a long time and have been kept from gross sins have a great deal to be humbly thankful for, but nothing to proudly boast about . . . Some good people tend to be caught up in this fault; they look down on those who have not kept their reputation as clean as they have, even when those who have soiled themselves in this way have given good evidence of their repentance and reformation . . . We have too high an opinion of ourselves if we cannot find it in our hearts to receive those whom God has received."

Henry continues, "If we are true believers, all that God is and all that he has are ours, and if others come to be true believers, all that he is and all that he has are theirs too, and yet we have no less."

The parable in Luke ends with the father assuring his oldest son, "You are always with me, and everything I have is yours. But we had to celebrate and be glad, because this brother of yours was dead and is alive again; he was lost and is found."

Oh how I wish there were more to the story!! I want to know if the oldest son embraced his brother. If his heart softened. If they had a "happily ever after!"

Know what? I have to believe that's exactly what happened. It may be no use to speculate, but it makes my heart happy to think they did get their happily ever after.

When those brothers saw each other the first time, I can't help but think the youngest brother, full of remorse, newly redeemed, and humbled to the bone, made a huge impact on his older brother.

And with a father who, by the way, should win Parent of the Year—gently, lovingly, and humbly came alongside the oldest boy to speak truth into him. He didn't shame that boy, or pull the "parent" because-I-said-so card. Instead he gently shined truth into the situation.

I've heard this parable countless times throughout my life, but the study, research, and revelation I've just experienced will stay with me a lifetime.

These three men have taught me so many lessons. Who I mirror, who I've been, and who I want to be.

Forgiveness Is
an Act of Faith
{day thirty}

To be able to look into God's face, and know with the knowledge

of faith that there is nothing between the soul and Him,

is to experience the fullest peace the soul can know.

Whatever else pardon may be, it is above all things admission

into full fellowship with God.

~ Charles H. Brent

Forgiveness is an act of faith, trusting God will bring freedom and allow healing, both in our lives and in the lives of others.

Forgiveness is an act of faith, believing God has commanded us to forgive.

Forgiveness is an act of faith, trusting God will work in our situations.

Forgiveness is an act of faith, allowing us to release our holds on each situation knowing God has greater plans.

Forgiveness is an act of faith, knowing God will handle any justice, mercy, or grace that needs to take place.

Forgiveness is an act of faith, trusting God will give us the power to forgive.

Forgiveness is an act of faith, trusting God will replace unforgiveness with peace.

Forgiveness is an act of faith, believing Jesus was sacrificed for our sins so we could live forgiven.

Forgiveness is an act of faith, when we choose to love instead of hate.

Forgiveness is an act of faith, when we pray blessings over those who persecute us.

Forgiveness is an act of faith, trusting redemption is probable.

Forgiveness is an act of faith, believing we'll hold no record of wrongdoings.

Forgiveness is an act of faith, realizing it's a gift money can't buy.

Forgiveness is an act of faith, forgiving seven times seventy.

Forgiveness is an act of faith, knowing there's no other option.

Forgiveness is an act of faith, believing in God's unconditional, unending, and unfathomable love for us.

Forgiveness is an act of faith, believing forgiveness will bring us into full fellowship with God.

How Do We Know We've Forgiven?
{day thirty-one}

When God forgives, there is an immediate and

complete change in relationship.

Instead of hostility, there is love and acceptance.

Instead of enmity, there is friendship.

~ Billy Graham

In the deepest depths of our heart and soul, can we say we've truly forgiven someone?

A quick check might be to ask ourselves, "What does Jesus see?"

When my girls have misbehaved and try to cover it up with a lie, I ask them one simple question, not in judgment or condemnation—they don't even need to give me an answer. The question is this, "What did Jesus see?" The fact is, it doesn't matter if I know the truth or not, what's important is they keep their hearts pure before the Lord.

Only God knows our hearts.

If Jesus were to look into our hearts, would He see true forgiveness?

Granted, forgiveness doesn't always happen overnight. In most situations, forgiveness comes in stages and there's nothing wrong with that. God knows our hearts and our heart-motives.

So then, how do we know when we've truly forgiven?

Following are a few things to keep in mind:

- **When we can wholly give the situation over to God.**
  Because let's face it, sometimes we want to hold onto it and play it over and over in our minds. We want to talk about it, justify ourselves, and prove our point.

- **When we can follow the command found in Matthew 5:44, "But I say to you, love your enemies. Pray for those who hurt you."**
  Personally, I've been guilty of this. When an offense has happened to me, I don't always immediately want to pray blessings over them and love them. But I know true forgiveness has come when the prayers finally come.

- **We stop thinking about it. We forget the crime.**
  All I have to say is—thank goodness God doesn't remember our transgressions. If He brought to mind every sin in my life over and over again . . . well let's just say it would be a sorry life to live.

- **Spiritually, an unexplainable peace finds its way into our hearts and minds.**

- **Physically, it feels as though a burden has been lifted.**
  I have multiple sclerosis and when I'm under the stress of a situation needing me to look through the eyes of grace, my symptoms start to flare. The worry and stress cause a physical reaction in my body. When I've truly forgiven, I feel a literal physical change in my body.

- **Finally, I believe true forgiveness has come when we see the offender and can wish him/her well.**

Father, I thank You—from the depths of my soul I thank You—for putting this series topic on my heart to write and share with others.

Thank you for your great Word and lessons. Thank you for your sacrifice. Thank you for being the perfect model of forgiveness. Thank you for the work you've done in our lives through this series.

Father, I pray lives are changed. I'm praying for a break-through for everyone who reads these words. I pray Lord we trust you with our everything and know You'll be faithful, loving, and just.

In Your mighty name I pray,

Amen

He Deserves What's Coming to Him
{bonus chapter one}

We want justice for others, mercy for ourselves.

~ David Hawkins

"He deserves what's coming to him!" Oh friends, a statement like that will put us on a fast-moving, slippery slope to nowhere.

I cringe when I hear words like these. I absolutely understand there are people in this world who do horrific and unthinkable things. Truly unimaginable.

We could never-ever-never conceive of doing something so monstrous as rape, murder, abuse, or some of the other heinous crimes being committed.

But.

Judgment isn't ours to make.

I understand a man may have taken the life of a loved one and we're robbed of precious time we thought we'd have.

I understand someone may have taken away the innocence of your childhood and you're left with scars so deep you're still nursing them.

But.

Judgment isn't ours to make.

> *You, therefore, have no excuse, you who pass judgment on someone else,*
>
> *for **at whatever point you judge the other, you are condemning yourself,***
>
> *because you who pass judgment do the same things.*
>
> *Romans 2:1 {NIV, emphasis mine}*

> *You, then, why do you judge your brother?*
>
> *Or why do you look down on your brother?*
>
> *For we will all stand before God's judgment seat.*
>
> *Romans 14:10 {NIV}*

> *Therefore let us stop passing judgment on one another.*
>
> *Instead, make up your mind not to put any stumbling*
>
> *block or obstacle in your brother's way.*
>
> *Romans 14:13 {NIV}*

God is the only one who can determine what someone "has coming to him."

When we make hateful statements "hoping someone gets what she deserves," two things happen:

1. **Our anger and hatred toward the transgressor cause us to sin.**
   And don't sin by letting anger control you. Ephesians 4:26 {NLT}

Anyone who hates another brother or sister is really a murderer at heart. 1 John 3:15 {NLT}

2. *We will be judged in the same way we're judging.*
   Let's explore Romans 2:1 and the verses that follow. "You, therefore, have no excuse, you who pass judgment on someone else." Catch that? No excuse. You have no excuse to judge others.

   "For whatever point you judge the other, you are condemning yourself, because you who pass judgment do the same things." Catch that? When you judge, you're condemning yourself.

   In verses 3 and 4 we read ". . . do you think you will escape God's judgment? Or do you show contempt for the riches of his kindness . . . ?"

   And verses 5-8 from The Message, "You're not getting by with anything. Every refusal and avoidance of God adds fuel to the fire. The day is coming when it's going to blaze hot and high, God's fiery and righteous judgment. Make no mistake: In the end you get what's coming to you—Real Life for those who work on God's side, but to those who insist on getting their own way and take the path of least resistance, Fire!"

Yikes! Throughout this series we've looked at many Scriptures and commands telling us to live like Jesus. Imitate Him. Love like Him. Forgive like Him.

This isn't easy stuff. I understand that. At my very core, I promise you, I get it! But it all goes back to everything we've learned and talked about.

- We are called to follow the way of life God has set

131

before us.

- With God's help, by releasing our vengeful and hateful feelings, we gain freedom.

- When we release these feelings, it allows God to bring redemption to someone hurting deeper than us.

Redemption
{bonus chapter two}

When the Bible says that you have been redeemed,

it means that you have been absolutely freed,

fully released, and totally delivered from all

that had you bound in the past.

~ Roy Lessin

As an extension of yesterday's message, today I'd like to discuss redemption. Allow me a few minutes to get all Bible-geeky on you? I've spent quite a bit of time studying the original Greek language of the word redemption and have lots to share!

As I've been studying, I've discovered there are two sides to redemption—redemption for us, and redemption for our transgressor.

In the original language {which I'll go into detail a little later}, the word "redemption" means to loose what is bound; it's the payment of a price to ransom; to release or buy back.

Waaaay back in the day of slavery, people would buy a slave for the sole purpose of setting him free. So this word, redemption, was used as a term meaning "ransom or price paid, to release (of someone from the power of someone else), to buy back or deliver one from a situation in which one is powerless to liberate themselves from or for which the penalty was so costly they could never hope to pay the ransom price. In other words, the idea of redemption is deliverance or release by payment of a ransom."[4]

As Christians, we know the word "redemption" means salvation and a freeing of our {confessed} sins. Christ's blood paid a ransom for us, for our sin. Just as the slaves were powerless to purchase their own freedom, we too are powerless to pay our own debt of a sinful life. Jesus paid our ransom and delivered us into freedom.

I've found four other Greek meanings to our English translation of redemption:

"*apolytrōsis* from *apo* = marker of dissociation or separation + lutroo = to redeem <> from lútron = ransom <> from lúo = loosen what is bound, loose any person tied or fastened is the payment of a price to ransom (lutron = money for a ransom = ransom or price paid for a slave who is then set free)."[5]

Exagorazo
to redeem
by payment of a price **to recover from the power of another**, to ransom, buy off
to buy up, to buy up for one's self, for one's use
to make wise and sacred use of every opportunity for doing good, so that zeal and well doing are as it were the purchase money by which we make the time our own

Lutroo
to release on receipt of ransom
to redeem, **liberate** by payment of ransom
to cause **to be released** to one's self by payment of a ransom
to deliver: from evils of every kind, internal and external

Lutrosis
a ransoming, redemption
deliverance, especially from the penalty of sin
134

As I look at these definitions, I can't help but notice the repetition of the words release, deliver, liberate, and this . . . "to recover from the power of another."

Powerful, don't you think? Follow me deeper?

Forgiveness allows us to "recover from the power of another." It's what we've talked about through this whole series. It's the basis of forgiveness . . . forgiveness frees *us*.

Can I take the liberty of assuming I have your heart on the premise of forgiveness? If so, can we take a look at the flip-side of redemption?

If forgiveness brings redemption, by offering it to our transgressors we're offering them a chance at redemption.

Our forgiveness allows our transgressor "to recover from the power of another."

Understand each situation is unique. Your transgressor may not want forgiveness or redemption. But what if she does?

As I mentioned earlier in the series, people who commit heinous crimes are broken, hurting people and are in need of redemption.

True redemption can only come from God, but can I offer this perspective: by offering radical grace and forgiveness, we can ultimately be responsible or have a hand in helping someone else gain that redemption from God.

When we step out of the way and release the feelings we're harboring, we invite God to come in and redeem a hurting person.

Everything in this life happens to us for a reason. And if some of the situations we've been through have caused us hurt and pain, wouldn't we rather have those things have happened for a good reason, for a good purpose?

Shouldn't we be using our stories for God's glory?

135

Generational Curses
or Sin?
{bonus day three}

To be living in any known sin is to be living in darkness.

~ Evan Henry Hopkins

Today I'll be piggy-backing off of yesterday's message—a message speaking to a deeper reason for offering forgiveness and redemption to our transgressors.

You see, if there's a possibility of redemption, redemption for both parties, there's a possibility of breaking an evil cycle.

We have an enemy who would love nothing more than to see an evil cycle of ugly continue in our lives, the lives of our transgressors, and the lives of both parties' future generations.

Quick example? The Hatfields and McCoys.[6] Seriously.

If someone doesn't call a time out, a truce, or wave a white flag, the ugly goes on and on . . . for generations.

Digging deeper still . . . if forgiveness, redemption, and ultimately God's light and truth aren't brought into a circumstance, the darkness, evil, and sometimes shame just continue on.

The topic of generational curses is a pretty controversial one. Personally, I don't believe God curses us. There is a handful of

Old Testament verses speaking to curses of future generations {Numbers 14:18, Exodus 20:5, Ezekiel 18:20, Exodus 34:7, Deuteronomy 5:9}, but as believers in Christ under the new covenant, I believe the words in 2 Corinthians 5:17, "This means that anyone who belongs to Christ has become a new person. The old life is gone; a new life has begun!"

> *Christ redeemed us from the curse of the law by*
> *becoming a curse for us, for it is written:*
> *"Cursed is everyone who is hung on a tree."*
> *Galatians 3:13 {NIV}*

That said, I do believe in generational sin. I believe if bondage of some sort strikes a family and that stronghold is never broken, it's quite possible the sin will affect future generations.

But I also believe when forgiveness is offered, redemption happens, and generational strongholds can be broken.

It's God's desire to redeem all things.

It's Satan's desire to keep us in dark places generation after generation.

When we bring the glory of God's light and shine redemption into a situation, powerful things happen my friend.

I've seen it to be true.

Father, this is a hard message. A controversial message. And I pray, Lord, our hearts are softened to the power of redemption, the power of forgiveness, and the power of Your light and truth. Father, I pray You light a fire within us to deliver nothing but redemption and forgiveness all the days of our lives.

Message of the Cross
{bonus day four}

The cross is the lightning rod of grace that
short-circuits God's wrath to Christ so that
only the light of His love remains for believers.

~ A.W. Tozer

The message of the cross? Forgiveness, flowing from God's grace.

Oh how I wish I could somehow write in a five-minute pause so we could take a moment and think about the beauty, complexity, sacrifice, and victory of the cross.

Can we ever really wrap our heads around this message?

In His very last moments, moments of sheer agony, Jesus shows us—in all His glory—He shows us the message of the cross.

Bible scholar Matthew Henry says, "Through Christ, even great sinners, if they are true penitents, will obtain not only the pardon of their sins but also a place in the Paradise of God."

On the day of crucifixion, Jesus wasn't executed alone. He was crucified between two thieves. One who mocked Him saying, "Aren't you the Christ? Save yourself and us."

"Although he was now in pain and anguish, this did not humble his proud spirit, nor teach him to speak good words, not even to his fellow sufferer . . . there are some who have the impudence to hurl insults at Christ and yet have the confidence to expect to be saved by him," Henry says.

And isn't it so with us? We expect pardon for our sins, yet withhold forgiveness of others. What arrogance.

But the other thief, in his last moments of death, his faith saved him. He rebuked the other criminal saying, "Don't you fear God since you are under the same sentence? We are punished justly, for we are getting what our deeds deserve. But this man has done nothing wrong."

Then he said to Jesus, "remember me when you come into your kingdom."

And Jesus answered him, "I tell you the truth today you will be with me in paradise."

The message of the cross—forgiveness and grace.

Christian singer/songwriter Nichole Nordeman wrote an awe-inspiring song, sung by Stephen Curtis Chapman for *The Story.*

"How Love Wins" has me completely undone. Completely. I admit, coming to the end of this forgiveness journey, I find myself spent and stretched. But this song . . . in so many ways it's the culmination of what I've spent the last two months writing about.

The song is written from the perspective of the second thief.

There are few words recorded between Jesus and the two thieves. And since death by crucifixion could take hours, even days, Nicole says, "it's a beautiful thing for a songwriter to wonder {about possible conversations and thoughts that took place between them}." And, "there was a lot of wondering that went into the song."

Following is a sampling of lyrics from the song, but I believe it would bless you so to follow this link[7] and listen to the song.

> *Love believes that it is not too late*
>
> *Only one of us deserves this cross, a suffering that should belong to me*
>
> *Deep within this man I hang beside is the place where shame and grace collide*
>
> *And it's beautiful agony that He believes it's not too late for me*

It's beautiful agony He believes it's not too late for me. Friends, it's not too late for me. It's not too late for you. And it's not too late for our transgressors.

This is how love wins.

Repentance
{bonus day five}

Repentance and forgiveness are riveted together
by the eternal purpose of God. What God hath
joined together let no man put asunder.

~ Charles Spurgeon

Friend, you may have read through this book not knowing the joy, freedom, and healing that is available to you through a relationship with Christ Jesus.

It's possible you don't understand and can't grasp the depths of what was done for you on the cross.

You may be living full of regret and shame for something you've done, not knowing the forgiveness you could be living in, and therefore you're not able to share it with someone else.

If that's your truth, might I invite you into a life of forgiveness and freedom, found only through Jesus? Jesus, who sacrificed everything so we could be forgiven.

If your answer is yes, simply pray the following prayer:

> *Heavenly Father, I come to You admitting that*
> *I am a sinner. Right now, I choose to turn away*
> *from sin, and I ask You to cleanse me of all*
> *unrighteousness. I believe Your Son, Jesus, died on*
> *the cross to take my sins away. I also believe He*

*rose again from the dead so I might be forgiven
of my sins and made righteous through faith in
Him. I call upon the name of Jesus Christ to be
the Savior and Lord of my life. Jesus, I choose
to follow You and ask that You fill me with the
power of the Holy Spirit. I declare that right now
I am a child of God. I am free from sin and full
of the righteousness of God. I am saved in Jesus'
name. Amen.*

Friend, if you've just prayed that prayer, please know I am rejoicing right along with our Father in heaven! You've made a decision today that will change your life forever! Congratulations!

Well friends, our forgiveness journey has come to an end. I thank you from the depths of my soul for journeying with me. I pray through these words, through God's truths your lives have been forever changed.

I know mine has.

Still stuck?

Read *31 Days of Forgiveness* again

and again, until the truths of

God's Word are buried so deep in

your heart that forgiveness

becomes a natural way of life.

I'd like to encourage you . . . if you've diligently read this series over the last 36 days . . . I urge you not to get stuck on one particular day, or one particular passage. I believe all 36 days are intertwined in this process. I hope you'll pray over them, asking God to work and apply specific inspirations to your specific situations.

Study Guide

I've put together this eight-week study guide to help you further explore and grow in your faith. I pray you take time to review, pray about, and answer these questions. And how wonderful if you could gather with a group of friends to dive even deeper into the promises He has for you.

Session One {from days one, two, three, four, five, and six}:

1. Spend some time in prayer asking God:
   - to reveal any hidden resentments, bitterness, pain, and unforgiveness.
   - to open your mind and soften your heart through this journey.
   - to work mightily in your life over the next eight weeks.

2. Spend some time writing down the people and situations requiring your forgiveness.

3. What does forgiveness mean to you?

4. Do you see a hypocritical nature in taking Christ's forgiveness and sacrifice from the cross, but not extending it toward others? Why or why not?

5. Which of the "forgiveness is not" statements hit you the strongest? Why?

6. Why do you think we're called to forgive? What's hindered you in the past to offer forgiveness?

7. Read through Matthew 26:36-46. In the context of forgiveness, what does that passage mean to you?

8. Take a few minutes mapping out a forgiveness plan for yourself. Look at your answer in question 2 and pick one or two of those situations. Then prayerfully apply these principles to your situation:

- prepare the ground—our hearts
- turn the soil—find out what's hiding
- pull out any weeds—unsolved bitterness and unforgiveness
- proper drainage—empty out ugly and replace with holy

Session Two {from days seven, eight, nine, ten, and eleven}:

1. What are your thoughts on Martin Luther King, Jr.'s quote, "He who is devoid of the power to forgive, is devoid of the power to love"?

2. In what ways are love and forgiveness intertwined?

3. What does Ephesians 3:18 mean to you? What "infinitely more" would you like to see Him work in your life?

4. How do the stories from days nine, ten, and eleven affect you?

5. Are we too quick to judge others? What if, every time we were to judge someone—throw the first stone—we, instead, took an inventory of our own lives? How differently would we live, and how different the world would look.

6. Do you think forgiveness is the language of heaven? Why or why not?

7. Has there been a time you've been called to radical love and forgiveness? How did you face that situation?

Session Three {from days twelve, thirteen, four-teen, and fifteen}:

1. Forgiving the unforgivable, is it something you could do? Or do you know someone who has, and did you support that decision? Why or why not?

2. Looking at D.L. Moody's quote, "I firmly believe a great many prayers are not answered because we are not willing to forgive someone," do you believe we can be barriers to God's work? Do you have a situation you've seen this to be true or not true?

3. What does 2 Corinthians 7:10 mean to you?

4. Have you withheld forgiveness thinking you'd condone a behavior? After reading day 14, have you changed your opinion?

5. Talk about a situation when you felt you were a "doormat" by extending forgiveness.

6. Explain the differences between being a "doormat" and extending true forgiveness.

7. Have you been in a situation when social media has gotten the best of you? Have you had to unfollow someone? If so, was your heart-motive pure?

Session Four {from days sixteen, seventeen, eighteen, and nineteen}:

1. If you're able to, take a few minutes to listen to the song, "Jesus, Friend of Sinners," and write down any words or thoughts that impact you most.

2. Could you say that you too are a friend of sinners? Share a situation showing why or why not.

3. What does Mark 2:17 mean to you?

4. Share how day 17 might have changed your thoughts on forgiving and forgetting.

5. Do you think forgiveness is an option? Explain why or why not.

6. Are you currently dragging a "park bench" full of unforgiveness, anger, resentment, and bitterness through life? If so, how could you move toward "unleashing" yourself and giving yourself the gift of freedom?

7. Do you believe you can love and forgive regardless of the temperature of your heart? Explain your answer.

Session Five {from days twenty, twenty-one, twenty-two, and twenty-three}:

1. Have you had to forgive someone again and again {for the same situation}? Talk about your situation.

2. Explain a time you've been caught in a hypocritical situation. Either when you've expected forgiveness, but weren't able to give it to someone else . . . or when someone expected forgiveness from you, but wasn't able to extend it to others.

3. Is there a situation in your life you're not able to forgive yourself for?

4. What does 1 John 1:9 mean to you?

5. What are your thoughts on what R.T. Kendall says, "forgiving yourself may bring about the breakthrough you have been looking for. It could set you free in ways you have never experienced before"?

6. Do you believe God has really forgiven you for something you can barely forgive yourself for?

7. Are you afraid to confess something to God for fear of punishment?

8. What is the difference between punishment and discipline?

9. Share your thoughts on Hebrews 12:4-11.

Session Six {from days twenty-four, twenty-five, and twenty-six}:

1. Have you ever wondered why Jesus had to die on the cross? Share your thoughts.

2. Explain if you had any new revelations when reading day 24. What impacted you the most from that reading?

3. In *The Peacemaker*, Ken Sande says, "Christians are the most forgiven people in the world. Therefore, we should be the most forgiving people in the world." Why do you think it's so difficult for Christians to live out this statement?

4. Is there something you do in your life on a regular basis to help you live the way Christ desires us to live?

5. Earlier in the book, when talking about "what forgiveness is not," I stated forgiveness is not reconciliation. Yet in Matthew 5:26 we're told to settle matters quickly. Do you see a difference between these two types of reconciliation? If so, how would you explain them?

6. "Anyone can love the loveable. But it takes a true Christ-follower to love and pray blessings over someone who hates you." Discuss a time you found this difficult, and a time you found it easy.

7. Why do you think the warning in Romans 12:21 is so important?

Session Seven {from days twenty-seven, twenty-eight, twenty-nine, thirty, and thirty-one}:

1. If you've been familiar with the parable of the prodigal son, in which ways did you learn something new in days 27, 28, and 29?

2. What are your thoughts on pride, greed, and idolatry, and how they relate to the parable of the prodigal son? How are those traits intertwined with forgiveness?

3. Do you believe God has no pleasure in the death and ruin of sinners, but He has great pleasure in their return and repentance? Explain your thoughts.

4. What are your thoughts on humility and repentance in light of forgiveness in the parable of the prodigal son?

5. What are your thoughts on the father immediately forgiving his prodigal son without one word of rebuke? True, pure-hearted, forgiveness keeps no record of wrongdoing.

6. What about those of us who—by comparison—need no repentance? Have you had to stand by and watch an "undeserving" prodigal receive the fattened calf? How did that affect you?

7. What lessons have the three men in this parable taught you? Who you mirror, who you've been, and who you want to be?

8. Which of the "acts of faith" in day 30 is the hardest for you? Which is the easiest?

9. Given everything you've read and learned, how will you know if you've truly forgiven someone?

Session Eight {from bonus days one, two, three, four, and five}:

1. "He deserves what's coming to him!" How do those words affect you?

2. What are your thoughts on Ephesians 4:26, 1 John 3:15, and Romans 2:1-8?

3. What does redemption mean to you?

4. Do you believe in the redemption of forgiveness? For yourself? And for your transgressor? Explain your thoughts.

5. Are you using your story for God's glory? If so, how? If not, why?

6. Do you believe in generational curses or sin? Go deep and explain your thoughts.

7. How do you think generational sin and redemption might be intertwined?

8. Do you think it's an act of arrogance when we expect pardon for our sins, yet withhold forgiveness of others? What are your thoughts on that?

9. The message of the cross—forgiveness flowing from God's grace—this is how love wins. Do you believe it?

10. In what ways has 31 Days of Forgiveness changed your life?

Scriptures on Forgiveness, Love, and Judgment

I'd like to encourage you to spend some time with the following Scriptures. Don't gulp them down in one sitting, spend some time sipping and savoring each verse. Open your Bibles, find each verse, highlight them, and take notes in the margin. Maybe one or two will speak loudly . . . if so I encourage you to memorize them. Let these verses speak to you. Let God reveal His truths through each word you read. All verses are taken from the New Living Translation.

But if we confess our sins to him, he is faithful and just to forgive us our sins and to cleanse us from all wickedness. *1 John 1:9*

God blesses those who work for peace, for they will be called the children of God. God blesses those who are persecuted for doing right, for the Kingdom of Heaven is theirs. God blesses you when people mock you and persecute you and lie about you and say all sorts of evil things against you because you are my followers. Be happy about it! Be very glad! For a great reward awaits you in heaven. And remember, the ancient prophets were persecuted in the same way. *Matthew 5:9-12*

But I say, love your enemies! Pray for those who persecute you! *Matthew 5:44*

And forgive us our sins, as we have forgiven those who sin against us. *Matthew 6:12*

Then Peter came to him and asked, "Lord, how often should I forgive someone who sins against me? Seven times?" "No, not seven times," Jesus replied, "but seventy times seven!" *Matthew 18:21-22*

When you are praying, if you are angry with someone, forgive him so that your Father in heaven will also forgive your sins. But if you don't forgive other people, then your Father in heaven will not forgive your sins." *Mark 11:25-26 {NCV}*

But God showed his great love for us by sending Christ to die for us while we were still sinners. *Romans 5:8*

Love your enemies! Do good to them. Lend to them without expecting to be repaid. Then your reward from heaven will be very great, and you will truly be acting as children of the Most High, for he is kind to those who are unthankful and wicked. You must be compassionate, just as your Father is compassionate. Do not judge others, and you will not be judged. Do not condemn others, or it will all come back against you. Forgive others, and you will be forgiven. *Luke 6:35-37*

If you forgive those who sin against you, your heavenly Father will forgive you. But if you refuse to forgive others, your Father will not forgive your sins. *Matthew 6:14-15*

And forgive us our sins, for we ourselves also forgive everyone who is indebted to us. And lead us not into temptation. *Luke 11:4*

So watch yourselves! "If another believer sins, rebuke that person; then if there is repentance, forgive. Even if that person wrongs you seven times a day and each time turns again and asks forgiveness, you must forgive." *Luke 17:3-4*

For you will be treated as you treat others. The standard you use in judging is the standard by which you will be judged. "And why worry about a speck in your friend's eye when you have a log in your own? 4 How can you think of saying to your friend, 'Let me help you get rid of that speck in your eye,' when you can't see past the log in your own eye? Hypocrite! First get rid of the log in your own eye; then you will see well enough to deal with the speck in your friend's eye. *Matthew 7:2-5*

Jesus said, "Father, forgive them, for they don't know what they are doing." And the soldiers gambled for his clothes by throwing dice. *Luke 23:34*

Don't just pretend to love others. Really love them. Hate what is wrong. Hold tightly to what is good. Love each other with genuine affection, and take delight in honoring each other. *Romans 12:9-10*

Instead, "If your enemies are hungry, feed them. If they are thirsty, give them something to drink. In doing this, you will heap burning coals of shame on their heads." Don't let evil conquer you, but conquer evil by doing good. *Romans 12:20-21*

Accept other believers who are weak in faith, and don't argue with them about what they think is right or wrong. *Romans 14:1*

Dear children, let's not merely say that we love each other; let us show the truth by our actions. *1 John 3:18*

Love is patient and kind. Love is not jealous or boastful or proud or rude. It does not demand its own way. It is not irritable, and it keeps no record of being wronged. It does not rejoice about injustice but rejoices whenever the truth wins out. Love never gives up, never loses faith, is always hopeful, and endures through every circumstance. Prophecy and speaking in unknown languages and special knowledge will become useless. But love will last forever! *1 Corinthians 13:4-8*

Instead, be kind to each other, tenderhearted, forgiving one another, just as God through Christ has forgiven you. *Ephesians 4:32*

Don't be selfish; don't try to impress others. Be humble, thinking of others as better than yourselves. Don't look out only for your own interests, but take an interest in others, too. *Philippians 2:3-4*

Since God chose you to be the holy people he loves, you must clothe yourselves with tenderhearted mercy, kindness, humility, gentleness, and patience. Make allowance for each other's faults, and forgive anyone who offends you. Remember, the Lord forgave you, so you must forgive others. *Colossians 3:12-13*

Most important of all, continue to show deep love for each other, for love covers a multitude of sins. *1 Peter 4:8*

Even to have such lawsuits with one another is a defeat for you. Why not just accept the injustice and leave it at that? Why not let yourselves be cheated? *1 Corinthians 6:7*

Anyone who hates another brother or sister is really a murderer at heart. And you know that murderers don't have eternal life within them. *1 John 3:15*

Resources on Forgiveness, Love, and Judgment

Books

Disclaimer: I haven't personally read all of these books. Some have come to me on recommendation, and some I've come across while researching this book.

Picking Cotton, Jennifer Thompson-Cannino and Ronald Cotton

Grace Is for Sinners, Serena Woods

Devil in Pew Number Seven, Rebecca Nichols

Total Forgiveness, R.T. Kendall

The Peacemaker, Ken Sande

Gracenomics, Mike Foster

Love Does, Bob Goff

Wounded Heart, Dr. Dan B. Allender

When Forgiveness Doesn't Make Sense, Robert Jeffress

Free Yourself, Be Yourself, Alan D. Wright

Let It Go: Forgive So You Can Be Forgiven, T.D. Jakes

Do Yourself a Favor . . . Forgive, Joyce Meyers

The New Freedom of Forgiveness, David Augsburger

The Forgiving Life, Dr. Robert D. Enright

Other Resources

People of the Second Chance {POTSC} – www.potsc.com
"People of the Second Chance is a scandalous awakening of radical grace in life and leadership. We exist to overthrow judgment, liberate love and live a life that rebels with grace for everyone."

International Forgiveness Institute–www.internationalforgiveness.com
"The International Forgiveness Institute is dedicated to helping people gain knowledge about forgiveness and to use that knowledge for personal, group, and societal renewal."

www.ThePowerOfForgiveness.com

Music

I'm constantly inspired and encouraged by Christian and inspirational music. I turn it on first thing in the morning, listen in the car, and play it in the house throughout the day.

I've put together a list of songs that remind me of the sacrifice of Christ, and my desire to live a life He desires of me. This list includes the name of the song and the artist who sings it, not necessarily who wrote it.

I encourage you to use these songs as walk your journey of forgiveness:

Seventy Times Seven – Chris August

Give Me Your Eyes – Brandon Heath

Forgiveness – Matthew West

Live Like That – Sidewalk Prophet

Losing – Tenth Avenue North

Give It Away – Michael W. Smith

Love Never Fails – Brandon Heath

Redeemed – Big Daddy Weave

The Proof of You – For King & Count

Love Is Here – Tenth Avenue North

I'm Not Who I Was – Brandon Heath

There's Only Grace – Matthew West

Forgiven – Sanctus Real

About the Author

Tracie is a redeemed child of God and momma to four vivacious daughters. She loves photography, travel, chapstick, guacamole, sunshine, crafts, pretty paper, slippers, and a warm fire. She's living with multiple sclerosis. She has her pilot's license, is a licensed barber, and owned stationery store, Broadway Paper (broadwaypaper.com) for 8.5 years. She has eight dogs {but wouldn't consider herself a dog person}, and is also the proud grandmomma to whatever creature du jour her girls bring home. She also has a slight phobia of escalators.

Tracie's mission is to encourage women to believe in better. She believes the Lord is writing a story within her. He's allowed her challenges and difficulties. But He's also equipped her with His love and grace. She trusts Him. She rests in Him. She believes Him.

In 2010, God paired her with a group of committed mothers of daughters to create the MODsquad blog (modsquadblog.com), a community of moms who encourage and inspire moms to raise daughters with purity, character, and hearts for God.

After a year of being tested and refined to her very core, in 2012 Tracie released *31 Days of Faith {finding joy in your anguish}* (31daysoffaith.com) where she shares how--with a deep faith in God and His plan for our lives--it's possible to find joy through any anguish.

You can find Tracie blogging at Tracie Stier-Johnson (traciestierjohnson.com) where she desires to show every reader the power of a living relationship with our Savior. She also shares fun crafts, parties, projects, gifts and on occasion shares a bit of her crazy. Tracie tweets as @tmstier and has a Facebook page at Tracie Stier-Johnson where she shares daily bits of inspiration.

The Favor of a Review

If this book has encouraged you, would you take a moment to write a review on Amazon? Ratings, comments, likes, or a simple two sentence review will spread the reach of this book to others who are looking to escape the traps brought on by unforgiveness, bitterness, resentment, and anger.

If you read this on a Kindle, when you get to the last page you'll see a "before you go . . ." page. It would bless me if you could take a moment to rate the book and if you have a Twitter account, if you would also choose to share the book with your followers.

I pray this book has blessed you and I pray your lives are changed in a way you never knew possible.

In Him!

Tracie

Endnotes

[1] http://www.amazon.com/Days--Faith--finding--anguish--ebook/dp/B0078HOIWO

[2] "Forgiveness: Letting Go of Grudges and Bitterness, http://www.mayoclinic.com/health/forgiveness/MH00131, Accessed 10/29/12.

[3] "High School Football Star Cleared of Rape – 10 Years Later" http://www.people.com/people/article/0,,20598633,00.html. Originally posted 5/25/12, accessed 10/29/12.

[4] http://preceptaustin.org.

[5] http://preceptaustin.org.

[6] http://en.wikipedia.org/wiki/The_Hatfields_and_the_McCoys.

[7] "How Love Wins" http://www.lyricshall.com/lyrics/Steven+Curtis+Chapman/How+Love+Wins/, accessed 10/29/12.

Made in the USA
Monee, IL
18 November 2020